AF478846

ARCHITECTURAL
MODELS

ARCHITECTURAL
MODELS

Ansgar Oswald

DOM publishers

Table of Content

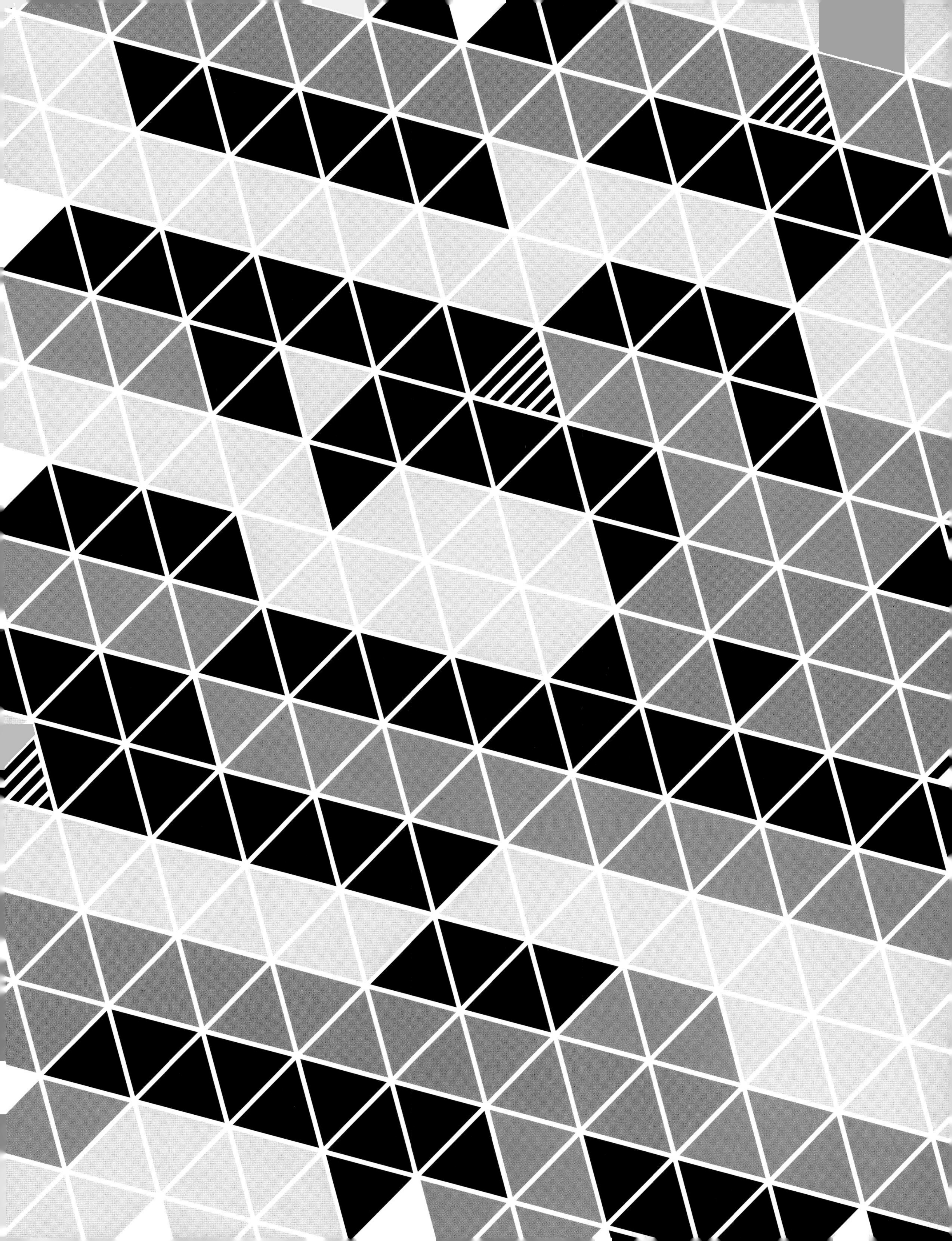

MUSEUMSHÖFE
WIEDERHERSTELLUNG FRIEDRICHSBRÜCKE

The First Structure
*Exploring the Nature of Architectural Models
in the Twenty-first Century*

Drawings and Models

Change can come silently even when it comes as irresistibly as a force of nature. Change can come in infinitesimal stages, so that it becomes noticeable only when, suddenly, nothing is the way it used to be. This kind of change occurred in the early 1990s, when digital design methods began their conquest of architecture firms and ultimately became the obligatory standard. Suddenly, architects felt that it was legitimate to ask why they should get their hands dirty when models of buildings could be created just as easily in the virtual space of the computer – and when computer models could be rotated in all directions and effortlessly modified if the need arose. Similarly, the value of drawing by hand[1] – a long-standing staple in the canon of design methods – has been called into question since the dawn of the computer age. After all, why bother reaching for paper and pencil when sophisticated Computer Aided Design (CAD) programs are easier to use and offer more versatile options for displaying and processing the results?

No advance in technology has had a more lasting and far-reaching impact on the work of architects and model-makers than the advent of the office computer.[2] This is significant because there is a close professional relationship between architects and model builders. Consequently, this process also affects ideas about what to expect and demand from architectural models – which, like the finished buildings, represent works of utilitarian art which have a practical purpose. Unlike hand drawings – which represent the architect's written notes, as it were, of his impressions and inspirations – architectural models are seldom created by the architects themselves. Architects who wish to present their designs to the public usually order a model from a craftsman who knows how to create a scale model from the designer's drawings.

It is the model-maker who is the first to give a palpable shape to his client's design ideas, and it is the architectural model that first conveys the architect's ideas to the public. Without models, therefore, architectural competitions would be impossible, and without an expressive, three-dimensional representation of the design idea, no architect would ever win a commission. Thus the possibility of using computer animation to turn sketches and designs into virtual models in an apparently infinite space calls into question the validity of the usual procedure of progressing from sketch through design, drawing, and building plan to the architectural model.[3] The virtual model can be changed with a few clicks of the mouse and without adding a single item to the real dustbin. It can be reproduced in many different ways and incorporated into media presentations. A virtual model represents an ideal portfolio for

1   Cf. Jonathan Andrews, Hangezeichnete Visionen. Eine Sammlung aus deutschen Architekturbüros, Berlin 2004.
2   Philipp Meuser, Fliegende Bauten, in Berlin-Stadtmodelle, ed. Senatsverwaltung für Stadtentwicklung, Berlin 2001, p. 12.
3   Cf. Christian Gänshirt, Sechs Werkzeuge des Entwerfens, in Entwerfen: Kreativität und Materialisation,Thema 4, no. 1, (1999),
    www-1.tu-cottbus.de/BTU/Fak2/TheoArch/Wolke/deu/Themen/991/Gaenshirt/gaenshirt.html (9th March 2007).

creating a haptic, three-dimensional impression of a construction project. The design, the plan and the model are all derived from the same data record. But architectural practice is not the only thing that has been revolutionised by computer-based design. The continual advances in computer science may also have changed our perceptions of workshop-built architectural models.

If this is true, one must ask where this change originated – and this question cannot be answered without examining the origins and purpose of three-dimensional architectural models in the design process. We must explore the intrinsic nature of the three-dimensional building template in order to detect the influences and changes which define its status in construction planning today. The technical possibilities in today's design processes and their interrelationships may have been predetermined by the intellectual projections of Modernism – the art and architecture movement at the turn of the twentieth century which by its very self-definition aimed to break free from everything that had gone before and to embrace something entirely new. In other words, this was a movement which not only displayed an intense focus on geometry and colour as fundamental design elements, but which also changed the contemporary laws of construction by using the physical laws of space and time, the infinite size of space, and motion as the fundamentals of its style and as ornamentation for a new, functional architecture.

01

The scientific discoveries that underpin these stylistic features are linked to epoch-making changes in the edifice of theory and the self-image of architecture and the city. Modernism, which is linked to such famous names as Frank Lloyd Wright, Le Corbusier, Walter Gropius, Erich Mendelsohn and Ludwig Mies van der Rohe, has left its stamp on the makeup of our architectural surroundings to this day. Significantly, this new way of thinking initially manifested itself not in the building industry, but in the fine arts of sculpture and painting. The new perspectives and the building methods that developed from them were tested mainly in drawings. Here the members of the De Stijl group of artists played a decisive role. Their clear, geometrical projections of form and colour into endless space influenced the architectural avant-garde, and especially the Bauhaus movement.

The *Contra-Construction de la Maison particulière* is an example of the group's influence on other artists. This work, created in 1923, earned worldwide recognition for its designers, Theo van Doesburg, the co-founder and spokesman for the De Stijl movement, and Cornelius van Eesteren. The isometric projection of Gropius' design for the director's office in the Staatliches Bauhaus Weimar (1923) adhered precisely to the spatial and projection patterns of van Doesburg's aesthetics. Its free-floating three-dimensionality gave the drawing a model-like character. Thus a new portrayal of reality emerged in the drawing, a spatial perspective which rivalled the three-dimensional model.

Models as Construction Templates

However, these spatial perspectives of depth were not entirely new. When, in computer animations by the Israeli designer Michael Levy, lines change into perspectives, combine to form grids and planes, and ultimately give rise to spaces and solid bodies to the accompaniment of John Coltrane's jazz album *Giant Steps* (2004), only to dissolve again into the construction grid, the technical steps involved in the process reveal not only the stylistic methods of the schools of New Functionalism. Rather, what the animations show is a digital version of a method of representing objects using a vanishing point and horizontal line which has been in use since the fourteenth century. Just as Early Renaissance drawings broke free from the flatness of the page by representing reality as it appeared to the eye, and just as they acquired space and depth with the aid of functional lines of projection following the laws of geometry, so these construction patterns became ornaments and art in their own right during the twentieth century. In the computer age, it is the coordinates of an image that constitute its crucial elements, while hand-drawn designs have become works of art and models at one and the same time.

In Levy's animation, the line is the fundamental element of every built structure – and even of the city as a whole, which is represented as a conglomeration of geometrical modules which at the end of the animated performance collapses into a myriad crystals. Thus the computer projections are an affirmation of a tenet that has been taught since the Early Renaissance – the tenet that the line is the basic motif of all being. At the same time, the projections refine and perfect this tenet, so that the structural elements, their results, and their decay back to their original state combine to form a closed system – a work of art. Additionally, the design possibilities appear to be infinite, just as the space displayed on the monitor is devoid of physically measurable dimensions. Everything is done with number scales and projections in which the drawing becomes the design, the design becomes the model, and the model becomes reality – a reality in which the real and the virtual world intersect and invite the viewer to embark on a seemingly endless journey through space and time. In the computer-generated images, investors, building control officials and citizens alike can experience the virtual building almost as a real-time edifice. This does not constitute an epoch-breaking event. However, what is new is the stringency with which technology perpetuates traditional elements within a reduced language of form, converting them into three-dimensional images which can hold their own against physical architectural models in today's design processes. Thus the constructed world inhabits a space beyond the dimension of the physically palpable, but also lays claim to the status of having been created with finite reality in mind.

Today's computer technology can bring to the computer screen fantastic new worlds which are completely indistinguishable from real-life environments. Elements that do not yet exist can be inserted into a photorealistic background which eliminates the dimension of time. And so the real becomes virtual and the virtual becomes real. No physical model that reflects a planned reality can rival these virtual models for authenticity. But the visual expectations created by these virtual reality images pose a challenge for today's architectural models and their possibilities.

Under pressure to keep pace with the pixelated bits and bytes of their virtual rivals, figurative architectural models must somehow try to satisfy the viewing habits of observers accustomed to, and spoiled by, the power of virtual projections. The suggestive power of the three-dimensional virtual

reality worlds on the screen is perilously seductive. And when these worlds become the standard of comparison for hand-built models, the temptation to add special effects bears the risk of betraying the unique characteristics of the architectural model. The issue is the more urgent when one considers that the conflict between digital and manual design practices begins at the earliest stage of the creative process, namely, in the hand drawing.

The Model – Idea as Matter

This conflict is a real one even though it has become clear beyond any doubt that the use of computer tools cannot compensate for a lack of drawing skills. On the contrary, the gift of putting a design idea onto paper with a few pencil strokes is a prerequisite for the draughtsman's sensitivity which is indispensable for placing a unique creative stamp on designs created from the menu options of sophisticated computer programs. The art of drawing is the ability to capture on paper what the senses perceive of the atmosphere of an environment or object, just as a writer or a musician takes notes to create a permanent record of inspirations gained from particular experiences. »The drawing is the language of the architect«[4], wrote Peter Conradi, the former president of the German Chamber of Architects, quoting Vincenzo Scamozzi. In his treatise *L'idea dell'architettura universale* (1615), the influential architect and theorist describes »the sketch as the germ cell of the design which reveals the creative skills of its author.«[5]

4   Peter Conradi, introduction to Handgezeichnete Visionen, by Jonathan Andrews, p. 7.
5   Quoted from Andrews (see note 1), p. 10.

Transferring these principles from hand drawing to model-making, one may postulate that the ability to convert a design into a preliminary construction/working model made of physical materials is a prerequisite for developing that unprejudiced clarity of vision which enables the architect to visualise the projected building. And this ability is indispensable for learning to assess and evaluate one's own designs.

In contrast, virtual reality blurs the relationship between design and matter and visibly interferes with sensory perception in that it tempts the observer to view the graphical image as the material representation of an idea. Hand drawing and manual model-making, however, are similar to writing: Using typographical writing systems – typewriters or computers – is difficult without a feeling for the shape of the letters which combine to form words and sentences and which inculcate a sense of their meaning. Applying this principle to architecture, we can say, »Model-making can only be learned by making models.«[6] This art is taught in trade schools and by architecture departments at universities. The practical skills, however, only develop in day-to-day working life. The old adage that practice makes perfect has lost none of its relevance.

While hand drawings stand in a causal relationship between observation and idea, the causal interactions in the architectural model are between will and deed. Many wonderful ideas were never put into practice because the construction model exposed the idea as illusory. Conversely, many ideas were never put into practice because they were never taken to the stage of the model. For example, Leonardo da Vinci created countless sketches and construction drawings for devices and machines – from lathes and cranes to vehicles and mechanical flying machines. However, because no models were ever made to determine whether

his construction ideas would actually work in practice, the drawings remained what they were at their inception: masterly representations from the pen of an architecture and engineering genius who also engaged in scientific research. Inverting this argument, we may conclude that it is the construction of a model that reveals the will to put an idea into practice.

To Change the World, First Develop a Pithy Idea This causal relationship is first documented in the year 1355. Sixty years after Arnolfo di Cambio began the construction of the Cathedral of Santa Maria del Fiore in Florence, there is historical evidence for the commissioning of a wooden model of a building. Although the building was fairly far advanced at this point, the work had been repeatedly interrupted and even stopped entirely between 1310 and 1331. The new construction manager, Giotto di Bondone, was not an architect and with the Campanile pursued an ambitious project of his own. In 1348, an outbreak of the plague in Florence once again forced an interruption of the work. To make matters worse, construction errors had crept in under a succession of different construction

6 Burkhard Lüdtke, Modell Architektur Design: Die Lehre vom Architekturmodellbau, Berlin 2002, p. 11.
7 On the construction of the cathedral of Florence see Andres Lepik, Das Architekturmodell in Italien 1335–1550, Worms 1994, pp. 27ff.

managers.[7] From 1353, when greater progress was made, it became clear that a model was needed to provide an overview of the future of this building, which was destined to be one of the landmarks of the city. The wooden model built by Francesco Talenti marked the beginning of a series of changes to the building plans, which were to give rise to a series of new models as well. This was the dawn of the rational methods of construction planning and management that has become standard practice today.

While this process looks perfectly normal to us today, at the time it was tangible evidence of the epoch-making process of social change that was to become the Renaissance. This upheaval took place at different periods in different parts of Europe. The perception of a cultural break brought about by the rediscovery of the ancient authors long served to perpetuate the concept of the »Dark Ages« even in the history of architecture. However, this idea rightly belongs to the realm of myth. The period after the collapse of the Roman Empire in the fourth century was built upon the cultural heritage of the ancient empire and its learning. Had this heritage not been handed down to subsequent ages without interruption, even the political developments of the following centuries would have been impossible.[8] There was simply no alternative. The time before the fourteenth century had access to ancient thought, thanks largely to the survival of the works of St. Augustine. Both Plato and Aristotle were known and read. However, the period owed its knowledge of the writings of Aristotle and other Greek and Roman authors exclusively to translations from the Arab world.[9] The lively economic and cultural contacts with the Arab/Islamic world also allowed the knowledge of the ancient world to flow into Christian Europe. Thus the cultural era of the Renaissance – itself a child of the Middle Ages – was dependent on certain preconditions. The change in building planning was one of the concomitant developments.

To what extent this change was the result of the reception of ancient Roman building practices remains uncertain. The historical sources provide very little conclusive information, and archaeological research into building planning and construction procedures is still in its infancy.[10] What is as yet completely unclear is the role which architectural models played in the building practices of the Arab/Islamic world based on its reception of ancient European and Near Eastern sciences. The influence of the Islamic world on European building practices is therefore equally unclear; however, the burgeoning trade relations between the east and the nautical republics of Genoa and Venice suggest that some such influence must have existed. In contrast, there is no dispute about the source of the inspiration for architecture as such at any period, including the twentieth century. The best example of this is the (unrealised) monument for the 3rd *Internationale*, which was designed in 1919 by Vladimir Tatlin. The monument resembles the mosque of Caliph al-Mutawakkil in Samarra (852), stripped down to its construction scaffolding and placed into an artificial pose resembling the Leaning Tower of Pisa.

It is almost inconceivable that the Romanesque and Gothic masterpieces of western ecclesiastical architecture could have been created without construction drawings and scale models. Our lack of knowledge here can only be explained by problems with the sources and by the negligence of researchers.[11] A recent monograph on architectural models in Italy by Andres Lepik is one of the first to

8   Kurt Flasch, Einführung in die Geschichte des Mittelalters, Darmstadt 1987.
9   Cf. Markus Hattstein, Wissenschaft im Islam, in Islam – Kunst und Architektur, ed. by Markus Hattstein and Peter Delius, Cologne 2000, pp. 54–57.
10   Cf. Lepik (see note 7), pp. 3f.
11   Ibid., p. 2 and elsewhere.

tackle the subject. A historian, Lepik writes about the planning procedures before the mid-fourteenth century that »there can be no doubt today« that »architectural drawings were in continuous use since ancient times«[12] both for design and for execution purposes. However, the only thing we know for sure about architectural models before the mid-fourteenth century is that scale models were not used during the design phase. There is evidence for the use of two-dimensional representation and modelled stencils as well as the so-called *paradeigmata*, which were used since ancient times for making standardised details of architectural sculpture in original size.[13] This is consistent with our fragmentary knowledge of a continuity between mediaeval workshops and the artists' workshops of antiquity, where both wax and clay models were used. Around the year 1000, the term *module* appears with the meaning of rule, form, pattern and example. The word *módulo* in the Vitruvian sense of half the diameter of a column first appears in the Italian language in the thirteenth century. In the sixteenth century, the word *module* appears in French and English to mean design, architectural model, image or example. But even this etymological knowledge, »despite a wealth of literature on mediaeval building practices«[14] does not constitute proof that scale models were used in architectural planning.

We see from all this that research into architectural models in history is fragmentary at best. The cathedral in Florence is the only piece of evidence supporting our knowledge that architectural models as we know them in construction planning and design today go back to the European Renaissance, which originated in the urban landscapes of central and northern Italy.

In the Model-Maker's Workshop In the fourteenth century, the urban republic of Florence was the leading power in central Italy. With its extremely wealthy and highly educated upper middle class, the city was predestined to become the germ cell of the Early Renaissance. The combination of an efficient and prosperous trading and financial sector with an unbroken artistic tradition since ancient times also made Siena, Bologna, Milan and the republics of Genoa and Venice – which traded with the Orient – fertile ground for the new cultural era. The economic prosperity of these cities expressed itself in generous patronage for the arts, coupled with the humanistic education and learning that was disseminated at universities and academies in these cities. This learning, together with the rediscovery of the ancient world, gave rise to the development of a rational political science and a new, pragmatic

Vladimir Tatlin: Monument for the Third
Internationale, 1920
Central House of Artists, Moscow
Photo: Philipp Meuser (2003)

12 Ibid., p. 14. On design practices before 1350 see ibid., pp. 11–26.
13 Cf. ibid.
14 Ibid., p. 4. On planning and building practice before 1400 cf. ibid., pp. 11–20. Also see Ludwig Heinrich Heydenreich, s. v. Architekturmodell, in Reallexikon zur Deutschen Kunstgeschichte, ed. Otto Schmitt, vol. 1, Stuttgart 1937, cols. 918–940, at 921.

statecraft characterised primarily by diplomacy. The prosperity of the citizens and the cities' desire for self-assertion both internally and externally together directed themselves against the Church as a political power. Only skilful diplomatic manoeuvring was helpful in this situation. The early apologists were Marsilius of Padua, Leonardo Bruni and Niccolò Machiavelli. Thus the Renaissance can be regarded as a sort of generic term for art as such, and also as the educational prerequisite for pursuing policies of urban self-confidence and sovereignty.[15] This phenomenon did not appear out of nowhere, nor was it limited to certain regions. Rather, from the twelfth century onwards, cities throughout western Europe began to reclaim, or assert for the first time in their history, their status as independent social, legal and economic entities and to function as counterparts of the ecclesiastical and secular territorial powers.[16] A middle class was in the ascendant in Florence, occupying the key economic posts in the Church – the biggest building client of the period – and asserting their financial and political claims on being given a say in construction projects. Design and financial competitions for building projects were held more and more frequently, with expert judges from the middle class choosing the winner.

Architectural models had the advantage over two-dimensional drawings because they made it easier for the observer to form a subjective opinion about the designer's intentions. They served as the basis for arguing about a design idea and for negotiating solutions. In earlier times, it was impossible to visualise the future building without observing the actual progress of the work on the construction site. As the architectural models used during the planning stages were miniatures of the future building, they

enabled decisions to be made before the construction work began. However, such decisions presupposed a conceptual awareness of the future, and plannability and measurability are secular, artificial norms dictated by humans. Architectural models represented »the first and only possibility of visualising an architectural project before it was built«.[17]

Moreover, the models allowed the architect to experiment and try out new design techniques. They were also used as working models for use on the construction site, to give an idea of what the building would look like when finished. Architects could then delegate the supervision on the construction site and turn their attention to other construction projects, so that the wooden models freed them from the obligation to be present on the site. For architects, the three-dimensional models opened up previously inconceivable business opportunities, paving the way for the division of labour between the architect's office and the construction site which remains standard practice to this day.

This new independence from the activities on the construction site inevitably led not only to organisational changes, but also to designs reflecting a new understanding of space and time and of the relationship of space and time to architecture. The advent of clock towers in the mid-fourteenth century provided the technical means of subdividing time according to the measure of man. As a result, human beings

15 On the relationship between urban identity, humanism and religion in the free imperial towns of Germany, cf. Bernd Moeller, Reichsstadt und Reformation, Berlin 1987.
16 Cf. Flasch (see note 8), pp. 117ff. Also see Jacques Rossiaud, Der Städter, in Der Mensch des Mittelalters, ed. Jacques Le Goff, Frankfurt 1997, pp. 156–97.
17 Lepik (see note 7), p. 9.

developed a new relationship with their surroundings, namely, the cities. All these factors must be considered if we are to understand the original social significance of architectural models. Together with other physical instruments that were developed during this period, they allowed people to move from belief to knowledge and discernment on the basis of the evidence of their own eyes and an independently selected point of view. Conversely, they engendered and fostered a humanistic view of mankind. Both these developments are clearly results of economic demands to participate in decision-making. The rediscovery of man as the *homo politicus* of antiquity began in the cities. They became the point of departure and the stage for actively shaping the cultural world to serve as a counterweight to nature. Ever since then, architecture – in its capacity as the furniture, as it were, of civilisation – has served as the backdrop for this endeavour, while its three-dimensional reduction, the model, represents the template.

The study of Vitruvius' *De architectura libri decem* was crucial for the development of architecture. Vitruvius, a Roman engineer and military technician of the first century B.C., provided the mathematical arguments for an economic society geared towards planning its daily life – including architectural competitions – according to the rational criteria of cost and benefit. However, Vitruvius makes his economic points because of his artistic aspirations, not in spite of them. In his view, economic viability and sophisticated artistic standards are two interlinked criteria for evaluating the quality of one and the same object. The value of Vitruvius' work of architectural theory, which came to serve as a kind of manifesto for the Renaissance, can hardly be overestimated as a source for the time.[18] His elaborations must have echoed the sensitivities of the artistic and social avant-gardes of the time so exactly that they were inspired to create something new.

Together with his laws of proportion, Vitruvius conveys the educational ideal of the architect as a universally skilled man – an ideal which was embodied in the Renaissance by figures like Leon Battista Alberti, Leonardo da Vinci and Michelangelo, who were simultaneously sculptors, painters, scientists and engineers. The architects of the time usually came from the artistic skilled trades. They might be skilled joiners or goldsmiths, such as Filippo Brunelleschi, who in 1420 discovered central perspective construction and used the technique in the double shell dome of the cupola of the cathedral in Florence (1418–36). With this construction, he created an unforgettable memorial to his own role in architectural history.[19] Brunelleschi consistently based his buildings on regular geometrical and stereometrical shapes. The architecture of Donato Bramante continued in this tradition. The works of these artists were a manifestation of knowledge, and the prerequisite for this knowledge was a new perception of reality.

New Perceptions – Space and Depth

The Architectural Model – Templates for Decision-Makers   What does this mean? In a letter to his family written in 1336, the humanist and poet Francesco Petrarca describes how he climbed Mont Ventoux in the Provence and felt that he was being »visually pulled into the newly revealed, yawning depth of the landscape«.[20] According to the philosopher of history Hanna-Barbara Gerl, this

18   On Vitruvius in architectural theory and his reception in the sixteenth century, cf. Hans-Walter Kruft, Geschichte der Architekturtheorie: Von der Antike bis zur Gegenwart, Munich 2004, pp. 20–43 and 72–79.
19   Ross King, Das Wunder von Florenz. Architektur und Intrige: Wie die schönste Kuppel der Welt entstand, Munich 2003.
20   Hanna-Barbara Gerl, Einführung in die Philosophie der Renaissance, Darmstadt 1989, p. 33.

Giorgio Vasari (1511-74):
Brunelleschi hands over the model of
San Lorenzo to Cosimo I.
Detail (fresco, undated)
Florence, Palazzo Vecchio
Photo: Bildarchiv Preußischer Kulturbesitz

first of the »modern landscape narratives« exhibits the same paradigm shift as the bronze doors of the Baptistery in Florence, where Lorenzo Ghiberti placed »Gothic absence of space and Renaissance awareness of space«[21] side by side on equal terms. »The acquisition of the body as a carrier of the self corresponds to the acquisition of exterior space as that which is objectively separate from the self: the spiritual interior gives rise to a new awareness of space which gradually acquires added depth in perspective – a depth which itself reaches towards infinity.«[22] This is rooted in the willingness to depict the world of everyday life as it really is – in other words, in realism. This new awareness precedes the total dissolution of the old worldview and the foundations of the modern, cosmic worldview, which was begun a century later by Nicolaus Copernicus. The dome of heaven that has been cracked, as it were, by science and the breakthrough into the spheres of the infinite universe are complemented by the empirically acquired knowledge of infinite space on earth by Christopher Columbus' discovery of America. The year 1492 became the key date in a process of cultural, economic and religious globalisation that emanated from Europe after that date. In the same year, the still-extant globe of the Nuremberg patrician Martin Behaim was created.

The model of the world and the architectural models are simply two different manifestations of the same process, namely, humanity's taking possession of the world by technological means. They are allegories of an expansion that begins anew in our awareness with everything we do, and which embraces the environment of the self. The former was originally an expression of the emancipation of man from prescribed doctrines which, on a social level, led directly to the Enlightenment and which culminated politically in the French Revolution of 1789. The latter is expressed in the birth of a worldview that places the world at the disposal of the free will of humanity.[23] This epoch-breaking event is described by the French philosopher Etienne Gilson as follows: »The Renaissance is not the Middle Ages plus man, but the Middle Ages minus God.«[24] And the architectural model was one of the tools with which man created his own order.

21 Ibid.
22 Ibid, pp. 32ff.
23 Cf. Gerl (see note 20), pp. 34ff.

The Coordinate System – the Measure of all Things   However, to master something in the sense we have just described presupposes the ability to comprehend and visually penetrate a space. Both in art and in politics, the constructed central perspective and spatial perspective became indispensable tools for achieving this. These perspectives developed in the Early Renaissance as the result of further study of the ancient authors. Artists like Duccio di Buoninsegna, one of the first masters of painting in Siena, Giotto, the Lorenzetti brothers and Brunelleschi were among the pioneers of spatial representation. In architecture, the development of central perspective was a precondition for model-making, as models represented a necessarily physical response to »the altered principles of spatial vision and development planning«.[25]

From then on, no art form was conceivable without an exact analysis of coordinates, reference points, depth and proportions that had been previously determined according to the laws of mathematics and geometry. All forms of spatial perspective, as well as the proportions of buildings, had the human body as their point of reference and point of departure. Columns – the elements of architecture most closely related to the human body – also played a crucial role. »Man (becomes) the measure of all things« (Protagoras), and thus he become his own model, as da Vinci illustrates in his allegory on Luca Pacioli's *De divina proportione* from 1491.

In the view of Hanna-Barbara Gerl, this new perception, in which man uses artificial yardsticks to categorise creation, represents the »conquest of space« as »a fundamental discovery in the service of artistic, intellectual and scientific development«.[26] This process began in the urban societies of northern Italy and changed not only art, but also everyday life throughout Europe. The Aristotelian conception of finite space which had been predominant before was now superseded by the idea of »infinite space that is independent of physical bodies and goes towards infinity in all three dimensions«.[27]

In today's computer-assisted design techniques, the theory of infinite space, which even Albert Einstein still saw in relative terms, finds unlimited technical possibilities of expression. Designs that were indisputably daring in the 1920s yet still created by conventional means, such as those by Tatlin, who caused buildings to rotate around their own axes, or those by Doesburg, can now be liberated from all the laws of tectonics. On the computer screen, they can be turned and shaped at will as bodies floating freely in space. Given the right materials, it is even possible to build the multi-dimensional spaces constructed according to the laws of mathematics, as has been demonstrated by such recent and world-famous examples of organic architecture as Frank O. Gehry's Guggenheim Museum in Bilbao and Daniel Libeskind's Jewish Museum in Berlin.

Today, fully-fledged master plans complete with virtual models can be designed on the computer according to scientific criteria and implemented in abstract architecture. The results, at first glance, have more in common with the laws of installation art than with classical architecture. Technically and scientifically, there is a direct line between this development and the mediaeval and early mod-

Jewish Museum, Berlin
Architect: Daniel Libeskind (1999)
Photo: Philipp Meuser (2004)

24   Quoted in Gerl (see note 20), p. 11 n. 37.
25   Lepik (see note 7), p. 10.
26   Gerl (see note 20), p. 31.
27   Ibid, pp. 32ff.

ern achievements of scholars like Copernicus and Kepler. Witnessing the influence of developments from Galilei to Einstein's theory of relativity on the architectural interpretation of the space-time continuum in the modern shape of movement and light, this process involves nothing more than the use of available technological possibilities and the implementation of theory in practice. Modern architecture therefore appears as an experiment – and becomes an experiment in art.

None of this is entirely new, as the example of Brunelleschi's dome construction shows. Since then, experimentation has been a fundamental characteristic of architecture – at least in the awareness of Europe – and a prerequisite for being able to bring forth something new. And the architectural model is the architect's laboratory equipment. The only difference is the technology that is used.

For the Renaissance, discovering the infinity of space was analogous to the journey towards knowledge in Plato's Allegory of the Cave. The architectural model provided a visual anchor and point of reference for this new experience of space, and its purpose has remained unchanged to this day – it is still the means that is used to provide a tangible expression of a new perception of reality. Since then, humanity has felt itself to be the creator of this reality, and architecture the most visible expression of the will to design reality. The architectural model offers the opportunity to experiment and engage in discussion as prerequisites for knowledge, which in turn can only grow out of a critical engagement with the object and which allows the designer to shape his surroundings independently.

Architecture in Pictures   This can be seen in paintings as well as three-dimensional architectural models. For one thing, paintings tell a story and also serve as a functional image of the idea of a greater whole which illustrates how architecture »developed into a spatial art which defined its compositions in terms of length, width and depth«.[28] Thus time is the only thing that separates Masaccio's *Raising of Tabitha*, van Eyck's *Madonna of Chancellor Nicholas von Rolin* and Raphael's *School of Athens* from Martini's work of spatial perspective titled *View of an Ideal City*, Michelangelo's Strada Pia in Rome, Fontana's Trivium in the same city, the design for the modified Fugger chapel in Augsburg and Le Corbusier's *Plan voisin* for the inner city of Paris. In terms of content the two genres differ only in their purpose.

What all these works have in common is a mathematical coordinate system. This system has allowed painters ever since to express their visual power over what they see, just as architects sought to use the architectural model to gain visual power over things that had not yet been built.[29] However, haptic planning models remained confined to individual buildings and details; large-scale physical models

28 Cf. Meuser (see note 2), p. 12.
29 Ibid.

were uncommon in architectural design procedures until the 1930s. Ideas which represent utopias in some way or which illustrate scenarios were expressed in birds' eye views and figures such as Otto Wagner's plan for the 22nd district of Vienna (1911) or the *Bird's Eye View of the Monumental City* in which one year earlier Bruno Schmitz subsumed several urban planning ideas in one design for the *Groß-Berlin* competition.[30] From the Renaissance until this period, perspective drawing had been used only in pictures of ideal cities or ideal urban landscapes, while architectural models served to illustrate specific individual buildings.

The Architect in the Model

The New Stuff of Art The shift in the practical value of three-dimensional models in building planning took place in the 1920s. Presentation models became more abstract – even in their details – during the era of the New Functionalism. Reduced to their basic forms, they revealed the influence of cubism. At the same time, this period saw the birth of urban design models like that by Martin Wagner for Berlin's Alexanderplatz. These three-dimensional reproductions were very formal in character and served only to convey the visual effect of the overall composition. Detailed representations of individual buildings continued to be used only in design competitions, true to the spirit of the new style of building whose main characteristic was described by Karl Hocheder as »progressing from the overall impact to individual details« (1909). In 1926, Adolf Behne said, »The purpose of the art of our time is ... to replace formal periphrases with functional solutions.«[31] Thus models were built in the same way as they were sketched – with great, sweeping lines. For example, the architectural models of Erich Mendelsohn's Schocken department store in Stuttgart and of the Woga complex in Berlin give the appearance of being simply a phase in the seamless transition from a contoured design sketch to a three-dimensional model. Everything was dominated by pure functional aestheticism, and new materials were used to create these models.

Previously, these miniature expressions of the vast will to build had been created from such natural materials as wood, clay, cork, plaster and metal. Now synthetic materials were added to the palette of possible construction materials. In 1909, the Flemish chemist Leo Hendrik Baekeland, who had emigrated to the USA, became the first person to manufacture a synthetic material on an industrial scale. His invention was the phenol formaldehyde resin known as Bakelite. The work of the German chemist Hermann Staudinger culminated in 1928 in the production of polymethacrylate, which is used among other things for acrylic glass, with polystyrene, another transparent synthetic which was inexpensive and could be used for spray casting, following in 1930. Once again, technical progress went hand in hand with the need to create new designs and supplied the materials without which the new forms of expression would have been impossible.

At the same time, and despite this preponderance of functionalism, the first three decades of the twentieth century had an unexpected sentimentality of their own. Model cars and human figures gave the abstract spatial models an element of realism which had previously been reserved for drawings and

30 Wolfgang Sonne, Ideen für die Großstadt: Der Wettbewerb Groß-Berlin 1910, in Stadt der Architektur – Architektur der Stadt. Berlin 1900-2000,
     ed. Thorsten Scheer, Josef Paul Kleihues, Paul Kahlfeldt, Berlin 2000, pp. 67–78.
31 Adolf Behne, Warum nicht schön? in ABC: Beiträge zum Bauen, 2nd series, 3 (1926), ed. Lars Müller, reprint Baden 1993, p. 8.

which illustrated the relationship between objects and spaces. For instance, Wagner's competition model for the Alexanderplatz features miniature vehicles arranged around a circular building in the centre of the square. The skyscraper designed by the brothers Luckhardt and Alfons Anker for Potsdamer Platz (1929–31) in turn is an impressive example of the new design materials. In addition to its meticulous attention to detail, however, this model also shows that atmospheric details such as figures to illustrate urban traffic were becoming increasingly indispensable features of solitaire models as well as larger urban landscapes. The model gave a three-dimensional view of scenes that had previously been seen only in drawings, such as the entries submitted by Emil Schaudt and Peter Behrens to the Alexanderplatz competition in Berlin. These drawings used shadow effects and expressed the grand design gesture in terms of horizontal and vertical strokes of the pen to create an almost photographic dynamism.[22]

In passing, these pictures provide a hint of this period's newly awakened enthusiasm for light and motion, which was also expressed in the shapes of the buildings. Ornaments were speed and light. And Modernism, which saw itself as the artistic expression of a new society's liberal philosophy of life, was interested in self-representation, and in creating the impression of a fresh, new mobility in the literal and the figurative sense against the backdrop of an equally fresh, new architecture. This was the message of the architectural model, too, for in the young but socially and ideologically torn democracy, conflicts and contradictions were initially fought out primarily in the cultural arena. The time of the Weimar Republic is arguably the first time in history that architectural models acquired a political impetus, though they did so not in a dogmatic sense, but in their artistic gesture. Cinema emerged as a perfect medium for showcasing architecture.

Metropolis – the Animated Model of a City   Three elemental ingredients came together here, namely motion, light and the architectural model. Together they shaped the pathos of a city driven by new energies. *Metropolis*, a utopian monumental film by Fritz Lang which began its run in the cinemas in 1926, affected the role of the architectural model as a module of everyday planning procedures in several different, far-reaching respects. While urban models had served in the past to portray (proposed) reality, this film was the first instance of a model representing an urban utopia – even if that utopia featured the building styles that were common at the time.

The model city, built by the film architects Erich Kettelhut and Karl Vollmer under the supervision of Otto Hunte, who was then the star architect at Ufa, was a pastiche of New York. The inspiration for the film came from a trip to New York which Lang undertook in 1924 together with Erich Mendelsohn. The film sets were full-sized, while the buildings themselves were shot as scale models. Pictures from the workshops show design engineers standing among the models and positioning objects such as trains and cars. Lang's film was the first to use camera work with live actors to breathe life into scale models. »Within the representation of a representation of architecture«[33] the viewer observes a scene which suggests that the action is taking place in the real streets and houses of a real city. On closer examination, the monumental city of *Metropolis* appears so perfect that it is almost impossible to doubt its authenticity. Even in 1926, the fact that the sets were nothing but a collection of mini-

32 Dietrich Neumann, Die ungebaute Stadt der Moderne, in Stadt der Architektur – Architektur der Stadt. Berlin 1900–2000,
      ed. Thorsten Scheer, Josef Paul Kleihues, Paul Kahlfeldt, Berlin 2000, pp. 160–73.
33 Ibid, p. 33.

ature models seemed disappointing and almost impossible« to convey to the public. This manipulated city was made possible by Eugen Schüfftan, the first architect to act as a cameraman and film technician rather than as a painter and sculptor. A technique named after him used mirrors to make the miniaturised architecture appear as life-sized buildings against which the live action could unfold. The principles of the technique were not new; even Brunelleschi was known to have used it.[34] But it had never before been used with moving pictures. This trick made it possible to replace the everyday architecture and to combine the model with a real-life environment, allowing reality to merge with fantasy. Whereas the model buildings had always before indisputably represented *idea materialis*,[35] the moving pictures turned them into the object of the production by such techniques as picture-within-picture compositions to create the illusion of depth. »One-eyed, unerringly trained on a single point, [the camera] appears to preserve objective pictures of perceptions.«[36] The new, Modernist way of seeing is analogous to film architecture. In films, the objects on the screen are at one remove from the haptic evaluation of the observer, whose perception is deceived to the extent that the architectural model fails to be clearly recognisable for what it is. This is the same effect that is created by modern displays of virtual reality on the computer, and has found its way even into computer games (for example, *Sim City*). The journalist and art critic Robert Breuer mocked the film in 1927: »*Metropolis* was

Tower of Babel
From the film *Metropolis*
(Germany, 1927; director: Fritz Lang)
Source: akg-images

terrible. Especially because it used toys to simulate giant-sized scenery. Skyscrapers that aspired to stratospheric heights, urban streets arranged in terraces one above another and packed with cars, thousand-horsepower vehicles going at breakneck speeds – all of it made of cardboard, plaster and tin. Models. Built and placed on rails by the director. And their effect: Constant oscillation between momentary belief in reality and recognition of the contrived deception. A nauseating violation of the understandable, naïve assumption that film reflects facts.«[37]

34 See Gerhard Vana, Metropolis: Modell und Mimesis, Berlin 2001, pp. 36f.
35 Werner Oechslin, Idea materialis – Das Architekturmodell – Instrument zwischen Theorie und Praxis, Berlin 2002.
36 Vana (see note 34), p. 39.

It was Mies van der Rohe who, in 1922, severed the architectural model from an immediate design purpose. His glass model for a skyscraper in Friedrichstrasse established a utopian dream in a real-life context. »Utopia, [however], is the construction of an imaginary, perfect world and therefore reflects dissatisfaction with the state of reality and a desire for change,«[38] art historian Henrikke Nielsen remarks about the nature of these kinds of ideal models. While models of ideal buildings were nothing new, nobody before van der Rohe had seriously considered the idea of confusing the ideal with reality. The ideal was something which one could strive towards, but never fully reach in the Here and Now. Furthermore, according to the fundamental understanding that developed in the Renaissance, the architectural model was tied to a specific construction project. Now, however, the special quality of a model was no longer »that it simultaneously exists as a physical object and transcends itself and the present time in the form of an idea with the potential to become reality«.[39] Mies van der Rohe's utopian skyscraper model thus attained »a revolutionary significance«, Nielsen writes, »because it changed the way one thought about (and subsequently built) architecture«.[40] Two things become clear here. For one thing, the model becomes independent of a specific, planned building project. For another, the model merged with the new technologies of photography and film and thus lost its solitary physical status. Both of these factors had consequences which can still be seen in architectural planning procedures today.

Modern digital presentations have internalised the new role of the model as Nielsen describes it – as the embodiment of a desire – and developed it to a level of technical perfection which, from the Renaissance to the 1920s, was confined to perspective drawings and figures. Thus the real caesura in the history of the traditional architectural model occurred when the division between the objective of a specific building project and the urban utopia – a division which remained clearly demarcated until the 1920s – was abolished. With the addition of photography and film technology, architectural models became a suggestive medium in their own right.

The Model City – Out of the Film Studio Into the Hands of the Despots

This occurred on a grand scale in the planning offices of Europe's totalitarian regimes in the 1930s: in Rome and, above all, in Moscow and Berlin. It was the latter two cities which represented the nerve centres of communism and Nazism, two ideologies which aspired to world domination. The urban design schemes for the capital cities of both regimes accordingly planned on the grand scale suitable for world capitals. The eclectic inclusion of Renaissance and classicist elements in these architectures prompted Otl Aicher to comment that classicism in general was the architecture of a centralist, authoritarian state.[41] Both Stalin and Hitler elevated the language of architecture to the iconographic vocabulary of a political ideology. The buildings became a grand propagandistic gesture, and for the first time in history, the model of the city became both the subject of urban planning and the arena for ideological games of strategy.

---

37 Robert Breuer, Der Film der Tatsächlichkeit, in Das Kunstblatt 11, no. 5 (1927), p. 177. Quoted in Vana (see note 34), p. 177.
    Breuer was the editor of Carl von Ossietzky's and Kurt Tucholsky's *Weltbühne* until 1926, but left because of political differences.
38 Henrikke Nielsen, Gedanken über Modelle und utopische Praxis, in www.sparwasserhq.de/Index/HTMLjan4/hb/henrikkeg.htm (9th March 2007).
39 Ibid.
40 Ibid.

No other country in the Europe of the time achieved the same degree of perfection as Nazi Germany in combining modern media with architectural models. *Metropolis* was no longer a simple metaphor; rather, from 1936 onwards, under the name *Germania* it became the embodiment of the will to transform cities in the service of power politics. The director of this political thriller was the architect Albert Speer, who was appointed by Adolf Hitler to the post of »General architectural director for the Reich capital«. Under his direction, the models were no longer confined to individual buildings and small districts of the kind that representatives of Modernism had built in broad strokes as early as the 1920s. The intention of using architectural means to transform Berlin into the world capital of a »thousand-year empire« which would be »comparable only with ancient Egypt, Babylon or Rome«[42] and would »outshine even the pyramids with its masses of concrete and colossal stone structures«[43] gave rise to the first full-scale urban planning model the German-speaking world had known. Architectural models as miniatures of whole cities represented both an anticipatory embodiment of political ideology and the architect's strategy table.

These gigantic plans, which were geared towards the population of Berlin more than doubling until the year 1950, required the use of scale models to keep the designers from losing sight of the overall picture. As their purpose was to provide a way to assess the aesthetic and spatial effect of the proportions and relationships of the proposed buildings to the city as a whole, the existing context was represented only schematically, while the monumental buildings were executed with a level of detail commensurate with their size. In this way, the models underlined both their proportions relative to existing architecture and the authoritarian aspirations of the new rulers to treat the city as a malleable substrate. The model was the three-dimensional counterpart to the general building plan. It left no room to doubt that the remodelling took its cues from history and yet aimed to surpass everything that had gone before. The gigantic north-south axis is clearly identifiable as the new, representative boulevard, and the great domed hall at its intersection with the east-west axis is recognisable as the new heart of the capital city and the nerve centre of power of the Führer's totalitarian state. The new functional areas – holding, for example, museums, educational facilities, sports centres and residential areas – can be seen along these two main axes.

The overall model had a purpose only within a hierarchy of additional architectural models showing environments, buildings and interiors. These models were built to the usual metric scales from sketches and designs. This rigorous execution of a series of models was a new development. At the same time, the desire for certainty gave rise to individual life-sized models and models of interiors and façades to illustrate details of the overall scheme. These partial models were placed in their destined locations like film sets. Some of them were so large that architects like Ernst Sagebiel had to climb into the model to explain the design for the projected airport at Berlin-Tempelhof. The Italian architect Pier Luigi Nervi, himself a specialist for monumental architecture in fascist Italy, commented laconically

01

Ivan Ilic Leonidov: Design for the Lenin Library
Diploma at the studio of A. Vesnin, Moscow, 1927
Model in the State Museum of Architecture, Moscow
Photo: Philipp Meuser (2002)

02

Model for a monument to Mussolini in Berlin
Design: Albert Speer (c. 1939)
Source: State Museum of Architecture, Moscow

41 Cf. Otl Aicher, die welt als entwurf, Lüdenscheid 1991, p. 101.
42 Karl Arndt, Georg Friedrich Koch, Lars Olof Larsson, Albert Speer Architektur: Arbeiten 1933-1942, Frankfurt/Main and Berlin 1978,
    reprint 1995, p. 93.
43 Karl Arndt, Architektur und Politik, in idem et al. (see note 42), p. 131.

on photographs of life-sized building models from the workshop of Speer: »Incredible – they must have gone crazy.« Everything seemed to have come straight from the sets of *Metropolis*, of which the Spanish director Luis Buñuel said that it turned cinema into the interpreter of the wildest dreams of architecture. Under the Nazis, cinema became a medium for interpreting specific design intentions. Another new development was that the different possibilities of a »strict neoclassicism« which grew »out of the spirit of the New Functionalism«[44] were so rigorously explored in the model-building traditions of the Renaissance and the new visual media technologies that it became »marketable« in the literal sense. In the work of the architectural strategist Speer, it became impossible to tell where reality ended and the dream began. In this sense, Breuer's critique of *Metropolis* reads almost like an unintentional critical anticipation of the merging of building planning and propaganda. In a sense, the architectural endeavours of the Nazis were really a film: an episode within a vast epic cycle.

The design of the architectural models was tailored to both these purposes, namely, to pragmatic building planning and to »marketing«. In this sense, Schäche and Reichardt are correct when they say of the Nazi state's architectural plans »that functionality and clear purpose were no longer mandatory categories of urban planning [and] architecture had become instrumentalised as surface design«.[45] »Since the 1930s, it has been possible to observe attempts to create an experience of space by using a dramatic vocabulary of images,« for example in the film *Raum im kreisenden Licht* (1936), which was produced under Carl Lang. »By using time-lapse photography, the film shows the movement of natural light in the course of a day in several Baroque interiors,«[46] writes the art and cultural studies expert Barbara Schrödl. Two years later, Fritz Terveen became the first person to »give a shape to the Nazi visions of architecture by moving the camera through an architectural model with extremely high and low viewpoints«. Both techniques were combined with a propagandistic purpose to create »the impression of a real, monumental architectural situation«. In this way, the language of film was extended to convey »the illusion of a spatial experience«[47].

The protagonists had the earnest intention of using the tools of urban design to transform Berlin into a cosmopolitan city comparable with London, Paris and New York.[48] Thus the Nazis went to work with a hitherto unforeseen rigour to adapt ideas which had first been seen in the mid-nineteenth century, but which had never been implemented or brought to completion, by elevating their architectural and urban design plans to the level of an ideology. At the same time, they defined and expressed their intentions by means of a hierarchy of presentation models. One aspect of these developments was the refinement of the architectural model of the Renaissance and the exploration of its full potential as the embodiment of a design idea.

Another aspect, however, was the intent to monopolise and dominate the citizens, depriving them of their rights as the true sovereigns of the state. Instead of stimulating the imagination, instead of

Model of the projected world capital *Germania*,
north-south axis
Design: Albert Speer (1938)
Source: State Museum of Architecture, Moscow

44 Georg Friedrich Koch, Speer, Schinkel und der preußische Stil, in Arndt et al. (see note 42), p. 138.
45 Hans J. Reichhardt, Wolfgang Schäche, Von Berlin nach *Germania*: Über die Zerstörung der »Reichshauptstadt« durch Albert Speers
   Neugestaltungsplanungen, Berlin 2005 (3rd ed.), pp. 43–44.
46 Barbara Schrödl, Die Geschichte der filmischen Repräsentation von Architektur, in www.gendernet.udk-berlin.de/downl/gzine3_schroedl.pdf.,
   pp. 3–4 (9th March 2007).
47 Ibid.
48 Cf. Benedikt Goebel, Der Umbau Alt-Berlins zum modernen Stadtzentrum: Planungs- , Bau- und Besitzgeschichte des historischen Berliner Stadtkerns
   im 19. und 20. Jahrhundert, Schriftenreihe des Landesarchivs Berlin 6, ed. Jürgen Wetzel, Berlin 2003, pp. 28–65, 102–176, 182–259ff.

functioning as the subject of debate, the models served to assert the state's authoritarian power even in the sphere of urban planning. The primary purpose of these architectural models was to bolster the dictatorship of the racially and ideologically motivated aesthetics of a state-imposed design canon. And this was a major contradiction to the nature of figurative architectural representations. The immoderate language of form with which the models outdid one another in size and execution and perfection symbolically underscored the unconditional will to shape reality. However, there was yet another dimension. The entire canon of architectural models was used to manifest ideas as built intentions – ideas which the idealists of taste from the Renaissance to the architects of the French Revolution had not dared to take beyond the level of two-dimensional drawings. The real insanity lay

in the attempt to cross the line between genius and ideological madness in the sphere of architecture. This objectification of a Romantic ideal was modern in form, but retrogressive in content. However, it was precisely this dichotomy that was the basis for the irresistible emotional impact – the same impact that even today's advertising strives for – of these models. More than any other discipline, it was architecture which expressed the distilled essence of the Nazis' ambition to present themselves as the heirs of European cultural history from the Roman Empire to the nation states. This ideological usurpation of cultural values was so total that it was bound to lead to culture shock. One of its consequences in postwar Germany was an unspoken official prohibition of a vocabulary – both colloquial and architectural – which had become too ambiguous after Auschwitz. In architecture and urban design, this was expressed in West Germany by a proactive move to embrace the International Style, which took up the thread of the Early Modernism of the Weimar Republic. The resultant functional buildings were bright, light-filled, airy, pragmatically free of ideological stuffiness, and radiated political innocence by their very language of form. After 1945, architecture and urban design were taboo. This might explain why the general public even today has failed to engage noticeably and rationally with the architecture and planning policies of the years between 1933 and 1945 and how they continued in the Modernism of the pre-war years and the postwar period. These issues are only just beginning to be addressed.[49]

Continuity in Change   Today, even Modernism has recognisably lost its socio-political innocence. That innocence could last only while it had an ideological counterpole in the Stalinist architecture which, as a kind of continuation of the heroic by other stylistic means, was favoured by socialist systems until the end of the 1950s. But strictly speaking, this innocence had never really existed. Many biographies of members of Albert Speer's planning staff attest to a seamless continuity between reform modernity, Nazi design ideas and the post-1945 reconstruction years. People like the »Reich

49 Cf. Elke Dittrich, Ernst Sagebiel: Leben und Werk 1892-1970, Berlin 2005.

architect of the Hitler Youth«, Hanns Dustmann[50], who had previously been inspired by the work of Friedrich Gilly to design and model museum buildings of Imperial Roman proportions, produced bright, airy architecture after the year 1945. As early as 1943, Albert Speer's »reconstruction staff« assigned architects to specific cities. In Speer's plans, therefore, the road from Berlin to Germania was designed to lead smoothly into a postwar form of Modernism. The changed role of the architectural model, too, was retained from the planning procedures of previous years. There were purely pragmatic reasons for this. For the purpose of assessing the damage in Europe's ruined cities and developing concepts for their reconstruction, master plans requiring architectural models of cities or parts of cities, which until the 1940s had been the exclusive province of totalitarian regimes, became indispensable after 1945, irrespective of political ideology.

Thus it was the 1930s which saw the birth of the series of architectural scale models enhanced by images which are part and parcel of the design and presentation techniques of today's architecture business. Moreover, these models are an indispensable part of the canon of democratic decision-making processes in urban design and architecture competitions. In the past, architecture became »the object of propaganda while still in the design stages and while still existing only as a sketch or a model«.[51] Today, in contrast, it becomes the object of propaganda in models and animated virtual models produced by the PR departments of architecture firms and builders. In other words, yesterday's propaganda is today's advertising – which means that it is now motivated by private rather than political concerns and has a more subtle impact.

Today, the interlinked practical value and propagandistic effect of the architectural model is created not by the medium of film, but by computer animations and multimedia reproductions in which the model increasingly merges with computer images to create a new reality – a reality which is becoming increasingly difficult to distinguish from real life, and which has a kind of life of its own. Architectural models made of wood, plaster, acrylic glass and other physical materials are now built to digital specifications using computerised machinery.

A Challenge for Tomorrow's Models

Architectural models have evidently become infeasible, both economically and from a planning perspective, without the aid of computer technology. A case in point, in the field of advanced design practices, are the models of the city of Berlin on a scale of 1:500 and 1:1,000. In 1996, a CAD architecture workshop was especially created for this purpose by the urban development office. Using an automated real-estate map, this workshop produced a digital site plan of the inner city of Berlin which is regularly updated with the most recent information. This CAD map represents the raw material from which the 3D model of the city was made. It documents the changing social and architectural fabric of the city all the way to the ownership records in the land registry. Out of a total of 2,000 land registry entries, 200 were used for the section of the city included in the model. Abstract in its contours and detailed in its information, the digital model generated from this data shows the different building

50   Cf. Reichhardt/Schäche (see note 45), pp. 48, 78–94.
51   Lars Olof Larsson, Klassizismus in der Architektur des 20. Jahrhunderts, in Arndt et al. (see note 42), p. 151.

types in different colours. The model provides access to information on specific properties and houses such as their addresses, number of storeys, building age, and residential demographics and allows the simulation of virtual urban development scenarios in order to assess not only their effects on the surrounding areas, but also interior changes such as socio-economic shifts. The animation helps evaluate the practical effects of changes in urban planning.

Computer data thus serves as the basis for forward-looking urban design and provides the figures with which the physical model of the city is regularly updated. This procedure ensures that the architectural model remains current and useful. From the perspective of the observer, the model represents a terrain which can be flown over and walked through in order to perceive changes and stimulate the imagination. There is an analogy here to Walter Benjamin's stroller, who walks through the streets to »read the city« (Peter Vahlefeld) and draws inspiration from the bars and restaurants, shops and all the other »everyday miniatures«.[52]

Model-Makers as High-tech Craftsmen As indispensable as computer technology has become, this Berlin example also highlights the exact nature of its usefulness and shows where its limits should lie. For the identification of those limits, Rolf Janke's comments in his monograph on model-making, which was the standard work before the introduction of computer technology, have lost none of their validity: »An exact impression of the city and its spatial structures is most vividly conveyed using

52 Thomas König, Die Bar als Metapher für die zeitgenössische Stadt, in at home he feels like a tourist, ed. Peter Vahlefeld, Berlin 2004, p. 37.

three-dimensional means. Therefore, models are used [...] to represent the architectural appearance of cities.«[53] What applies to models of cities is equally true of any figurative representation of architecture, even down to individual rooms as the smallest units of architectural design. It is always the immediate relationship of the unit to its surroundings that is at issue. The hierarchy of three-dimensional representations has developed significantly since 29 May 1355, when Francesco Talenti received the commission to build a wooden model of the cathedral of Florence, to say nothing of the differentiation into different model types, namely experimental and competition models. However, it is not only the developmental potential of the haptic model for which we have historical documentation. As construction tasks became more complex, the detail and variety of architectural models also increased – though the larger context remained important as well.

Technical progress goes hand in hand with the temptation to individualise the architectural model as a performance in its own right. Even the Renaissance masters occasionally succumbed, which may be why Leon Battista Alberti sought to impose rules for model-making on his profession in his *De re aedificatoria* (1451), a treatise as normative as it was groundbreaking: »Creating beautified models [...] is the sign of a high-flyer who wishes only to deceive the eyes of the observer and distract attention from the correct arrangement of the parts that are subject to evaluation.«[54] This comment by the Florentine humanist, artist and scholar has lost none of its validity. Indeed, it is more valid than ever in the face of the constant development of new visual technologies and their use in multimedia contexts in the twenty-first century. The physical representation is no longer the sole representative of the physical structure. Rather, architectural models – and the entire model-making profession along with them – seem to have come under pressure from digital technology in several different ways.

02

One of the pressures is logistical, in that the addition of computer simulation techniques to traditional design methods has caused »an independent, virtual world to come into being«[55] at an alarming pace: a world in which measured distances between the place where the designs are created and the actual construction site are no longer a concern. Designing a model in some rural backwater and presenting it in Shanghai is simply a question of high-speed connections, not one of resources. Thus architectural models are no longer strictly necessary. Three-dimensional computer animations can showcase dreams as though they were accomplished facts and serve them up ready-made to architects, competition organisers and investors alike. Today's project developers even maintain in-house departments which are dedicated exclusively to »building models« on the computer screen which are then used to award construction contracts.«[56] Time, after all, is money. The profession comes under financial pressure as well.

53 Rolf Janke, architekturmodelle, Stuttgart 1962, p. 27.
54 Quoted in Lepik (see note 7), p. 123.
55 Evaluationsbericht Architektur an den Hochschulen in Baden-Württemberg 2002, ed. Evaluationsagentur Baden-Württemberg,
    Stiftung öffentlichen Rechts: www.evalag.de/architektur.pdf, p. 12 (9th March 2007).
56 Neue Maßstäbe in der Architekturdarstellung, in www.architektur-online.com/archiv/Heft0703/Diva/Diva.html.

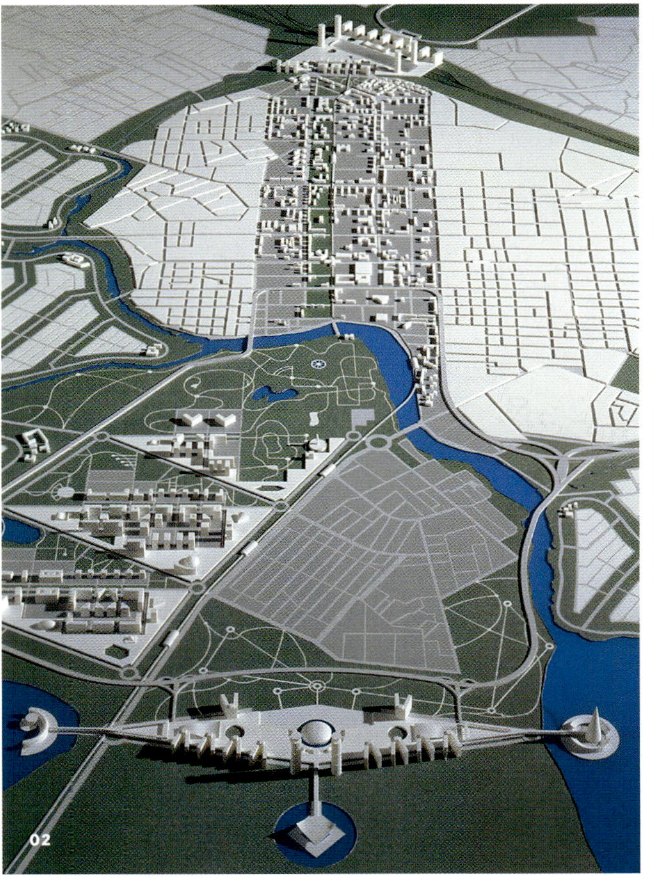

The finished idea is the template for the building plan. All this fits nicely into the concept of contrived, short-lived cost-benefit calculations, and it is not only the scale model that is eliminated from the design process. The entire discursive value chain, including processes of democratic codetermination, is threatening to break. The subject of debate is no longer a design which is illustrated by a model to provide an initial idea of a projected building. Rather, the discussion focuses on accomplished facts. Should this method become standard practice, the architect's artistic sovereignty would be at stake, and the model-making profession, too, would feel the consequences. Model-makers would instantly find themselves on the red list of endangered professions. Even now they could do with a bit of conservation concern.

The digital revolution in the architects' design and planning offices has gone hand in hand with another in the model-makers' workshops. Talenti was a craftsman who probably built the wooden model for the cathedral of Florence in the same way as he made furniture. Today, too, architectural model-making is usually only one of many skills in the model-maker's portfolio. The period when the profession of the demonstration model-maker had an explicit right to a master's certificate of its own spanned the years between 1974 and 2005. Measured against the timeline of the history of the discipline, this period was nothing more than a brief episode. But the difference between Talenti and other master craftsmen of bygone centuries and their modern counterparts is that today's model-makers have lost the status of skilled craftsmen. Ideally, they should have solid technical and tradesman's qualifications. Frequently, model-makers are graduate engineers with craftsman's training and qualifications in industry, design, technology and architecture. Increasingly, too, model-makers are familiar with digital visualisation technologies. They might be described as high-tech specialists in mould pattern building who are very

04

05

good at reading plans and able to convert them into high-precision three-dimensional representations. This new performance profile is largely defined by architecture, which increasingly assimilates the possibilities of automobile design or takes its inspiration from mobile shapes. The Allianz Arena in Munich, for instance, is essentially an automobile tyre turned into architecture.[57] In this way, the self-image of architecture as a discipline which, throughout its history, always grew out of the immediately preceding architectural epoch, is in the process of changing. For example, floral ornaments have

57 Cf. Dirk Meyhöfer, motortecture: architektur für automobilität, Ludwigsburg 2003.

become architecture in their own right in the form of organic shapes. Architects today are increasingly drawing their creative inspiration from the forms common in industrial design and the automobile industry. Even the grids used in rendering automobile designs on the computer have been elevated to the status of ornament. The possibilities for turning digital designs into physical objects have turned architects into auto-architecture designers. The model-maker's job description has changed accordingly, which may be another reason why model-makers should be architects, too.

The fact that many architects are changing professions and becoming model-makers may serve to confirm the close relationship between the two careers. At any rate, the one cannot survive without the other. Unlike 3D visualisations, in which a building storey suspended in mid-air may look like a daring idea or cleverly conceal a poorly thought-out design, an architectural model mercilessly reveals every error in the design. A good model-maker must therefore demand clarity of planning from his client if he is to build a physical architectural model. A well-developed working plan is a prerequisite for creating a model, because the model is the first constructed version of the projected building. Thus the model-maker is the first architect of the architecture conceived by the architect. This is what Gänshirt refers to when he places the architectural model at a point in the six-stage planning process that lies between the drawing, which represents a mathematical abstraction, and the calculation of the space plan, outlays and building costs on the basis of which the final verdict is pronounced on a construction project. Gänshirt therefore describes the scaled-down replica of the projected building as an instrument in which the idea can prove itself against the unavoidable cost-benefit calculation in an experimental

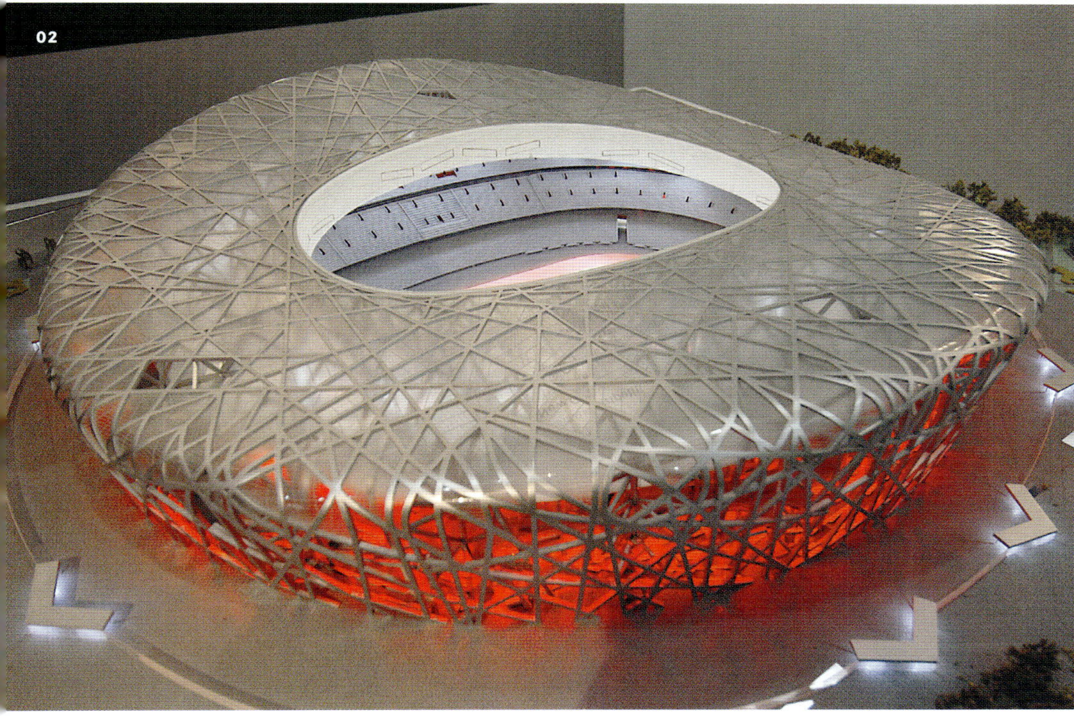

Model of Mercedes-Benz Museum, Stuttgart
Architect: UN-Studio (2001–06)
Photo: Mercedes-Benz Museum, Stuttgart (2004)

Model of Olympic Stadium, Beijing,
People's Republic of China
Architect: Herzog & de Meuron (2008)
Photo: Florian Meuser

form that is independent of the status of materialisation. Whether as a working model or, at a later stage, as a presentation or competition model, this confirms Ernst Rank's theory that »any kind of planning [also] requires a spatial model to create an idea of the object that is to be developed«.[58] Otl Aicher has pointed out the extent to which models have superseded even mathematical formulas in the design process, both in the concrete and in the figural sense.[59]

As the first architect in the construction process, the model-maker increasingly also functions as a consultant. This role gains added significance in that the entrance requirements for studying architecture do not include practical training in carpentry or bricklaying. Architects, therefore, are products of academic theory who typically have no immediate experience in dealing with building materials and how these are put together to make a building. And their remoteness from the actual construction process can have far more serious consequences than the mistakes that result from putting together an item from the Ikea catalogue without referring to the instructions.

But this is only the worst in a long litany of mistakes. The fateful process of alienation begins when model-makers complain that even many architects are as uninterested in experimenting as they are unaware of the fact that a physical architectural model cannot and should not be a real-life duplicate of a 3D visualisation. The common lament of model-makers about the diminishing ability of architects, clients and brokers to interpret an abstract model is a symptom of an educational decline extending to perceptual skills, which atrophy through exposure to computer images. As a result, architectural models are embellished with trees, figures and other accessories from toyland – accessories that look as though they had been borrowed from a model train set and which tempt the decision-makers to assume a playful attitude towards understanding their own designs. The art historian Walter Grasskamp

58 Ernst Rank, Produktmodelle und ihre Bedeutung für vernetzt-kooperative Planungsprozesse, Technical University of Munich:
www.inf.bauwesen.tu-muenchen.de/~niggl/spp1103/data/zwischenbericht_2002.pdf (9th March 2007).
59 Otl Aicher, analog und digital, Lüdenscheid 1991, p. 188.
60 Cf. Henrikke Nielsen, Gedanken über Modelle und utopische Praxis, in www.sparwasserhq.de/Index/HTMLjan4/hb/henrikkeg.htm.

coined the term »sentimental model«[60] to describe this trend in model building. Sentimental models are open to the charge of aiming only to look pretty in themselves. Their message is misleading and misses the true purpose of an architectural model in the design process. In his capacity as contractor for his client and final link in the production chain, the model maker is therefore frequently unable to be everything he ought to be for his client, namely, a shrewd, pragmatic advisor who independently creates the model as a »translation« and an objectified interpretation of the design idea. This inability may be the reason why today's models are frequently not all they should be. Another reason is the fast pace of developments today. When time is short, models are dispensed with altogether, even though this can lead to errors during the construction phase which may be expensive to correct. Pressure of time is the leading cause of errors both during planning and on the construction site. And the gravest possible error is the decision to forego a detailed architectural model. Past generations were aware of this, so they invested the necessary time in creating scale models.

Historical documents show that Talenti spent about a month on his model of the cathedral.[61] However, this was only a partial model. In contrast, Lepik believes that the model of the cathedral of Milan on which the joiner Simone da Piacenza spent six months in 1391 must have been a complete model.[62] Given the degree of mechanisation in the modern world, even outsiders cannot help noticing that the time pressure is disproportionately greater today, especially considering the many complex stages in the process and the quality that is expected of architectural models. The changes in the nature of the profession are reflected in the rapidly changing character of its products. Model-makers have become a fixed element of the digital economy and are subject to all its rules.

The Vocabulary of the Model: Material, Creativity, Form An escape from the »ever-increasing pace and pressure of the digital economy«[63] might lie in deceleration and simplification. However, this cannot be taken to the extreme of turning the model-maker into a rural woodcarving artist. After all, architectural models originated as the products of a process of rationalisation and mechanisation in the working world. At the same time, however, they are also part of our cultural heritage as the embodiments of ideas and the instruments of independent evaluation. But they can only fulfil this function if the model-maker is acknowledged in his natural capacity as a consultant. And consulting takes time as well as the ability to read a paper sketch and infer the physics involved and the materials required to create the building that the sketch describes. This is an ability that frequently provokes frank amazement from the model-maker's professional counterparts, such as architects: »Oh, so that's what it looks like! I thought it would be completely different!« Model-makers frequently find that the layman's first impulse after seeing the model is to touch it and feel its weight and the materials that went into its making. While this impulse must obviously be restrained, the Viennese architect Hiesmayr explains its origins in a kinship which is rooted in the human desire to achieve »model-like clarity about their own thoughts«.[64]

61 Cf. Lepik (see note 7), p. 29f.
62 Ibid., p. 47ff.
63 Peter Glotz, Arbeit in der digitalen Ökonomie: Der Kulturkampf zwischen Beschleunigern und Entschleunigern,
    Neue Zürcher Zeitung, no. 1 (2001), p. 33.
64 Ernst Hiesmayr, Der Mensch – ein Modell, introduction to Vana (see note 34), p. 7.

People in the Renaissance seem to have been more aware of this fact than their modern descendants who are in a position to decide the fate of building projects and, by extension, the living conditions of others. For Renaissance builders, the demonstration model did not only represent empirical proof of a plan's feasibility and the final stage in the planning process, but also offered an opportunity to experiment – and this opportunity was a crucial prerequisite for comprehending and refining a design idea. Alberti wrote that it was the purpose of architectural models to be »plain and simple«.[65] Details destroy that detachment from reality which is one of the necessary requirements of a model. Without this detachment, the limits of the human perceptive faculties make it impossible for the observer to arrive at an independent assessment of the model.[66]

Thus deceleration could consist of a pragmatic focus on the core design aspects we have just discussed; this would free the architectural model from the need to compete with the simulated reality of computer-animated projections. One of the reasons for the easy interchangeability of architectural models and computer images may be the misconception that three-dimensional models must be able to imitate the deceptive photorealism of computer-architectural sculptures to develop very swiftly into naturalistic representations. There is a vicious circle at work here. One possible way out may be to rediscover and use the unique language of the architectural model, the most fundamental vocabulary of which lies in abstraction and in focusing on suitable materials and their potentials for variation and refinement. The graduate designer and art teacher Burkhard Lüdtke uses this vocabulary in ways that are sometimes highly unorthodox, but always creative. He teaches architecture students to use ordinary materials to create surprising yet functional three-dimensional shapes. In this way, a partial model of a city is transformed into a study in different ways of creating identical objects using materials such as wood, Styrodur, stacked glass panes and metal. The range of interpretations multiplies still more by treating the same materials in different ways and by adding different colours. The secret of this chameleon effect lies in experimentation. However, Lüdtke points out that this process involves the »risk of falling flat on your face and wasting time«, something which has become almost impossible even at university and which »increasingly makes experimentation a luxury«.[67] Engaging with a project on the level of manual skills leads to experiments with traditional materials like wood, polystyrene and plaster and with techniques which are not usually applied to standard model-making materials.

Referring to the architect Günter Behnisch, Gänshirt stresses that the material used to make models has a retroactive effect on the design process. Every material has its own properties on a specific scale, while simultaneously pointing beyond itself. Materials have a crucial impact on the development of design ideas. Their nature represents a palpable expression of the nascent architecture. Thus it is the fundamental elements of spatial design – volume, surface area and line – that constitute the scaled-down image of a piece of architecture, expressing themselves, as Lüdtke remarks, in materials, colours and structures.[68] Every model-making task, from the abstraction of a landscape to the interpretation of classical architectural elements, offers a multiplicity of possibilities for expression. The only limits are those set by one's own imagination and the inherent qualities of the means one

65 Quoted in Lepik (see note 7), p. 123.
66 Cf. Vana (see note 34), pp. 19–20 and 62ff.
67 Burkhard Lüdtke, Modell Architektur Design, Berlin 2002, p. 11
68 Cf. Lüdtke (see note 67).

has chosen. While this sort of inventive energy occasionally brings forth some bizarre combinations, the main objective is to discover model-making as an artistic act. As one of the stages of architectural planning, this three-dimensional interpretation has a purpose distinct from that of sketches and drawings. The only professor of model-making in Germany encourages free-wheeling experimentation with materials and processing techniques to enable aspirant architects to gain haptic and visual experience of materials, to learn how to work with them and create objects with definite proportions. A glance around this model-building laboratory, which accepts commissions and thus straddles the border between teaching and everyday work, provides an impression of the variety of craftsman's techniques which, under pressure of deadlines, cost-cutting and competition from the digital world, are falling into disuse in the day-to-day model-maker's work. Lüdtke's laboratory produces such sensible »curiosities« as a model of the Berlin Reichstag building for the blind. A product like this may be the best option for rediscovering the fundamental vocabulary of the model, because a replica that literally helps blind people to grasp the concept of the architecture is easily intelligible for sighted people as well.

The core idea seeking expression is a fundamental feature not only of working models or presentation and competition models. A sales model, too, should have a message and confine itself to conveying that message. An historical model reduced to proportions and crucial elements will convey more than a highly detailed one, because existing buildings, too, have a design message of their own. The aim is always to enable the observer to understand the model and quickly grasp the main ideas of a design or an historical building. In this sense, the potential of all types of models, not only reconstruction models, is a long way from being exhausted. Most models are characterised by a timid conservatism, and this is especially true of sales and exhibition models. This seems odd because it was Modernism which, after the demise of ornamentation, took the stipulation of Alberti and other theorists of the Renaissance, that models should be simple, and applied it to architecture under the motto that »form follows function«. Architecture became schematic: the abstract expression of the principles of reduction and pragmatism which are typical of any model.[69]

69 Vana, (see note 34), p. 40.

The demand for ever greater speed and perfection destroys the main prerequisite for the development of a model, namely, the luxury of being able to engage with the design idea. However, model-making is a little like copywriting – thoughts that exist only in the mind remain vague and do not acquire a shape until they are put down on paper. Once written down, their sense becomes graspable, their value becomes verifiable, they can be weighed against one another and inspire one another, engender new creative thoughts, and collectively become a malleable and usable mass which is perfected in a text just as an intriguing model is perfected within a convincing work. Just as the text is the model that represents the practical applications in which its content must prove itself, so the architectural model is always the object in which the design idea becomes embodied at a specific stage of development and in which it must prove itself before it can ultimately become reality.

Precision is important. But quality in architectural model-making is characterised by a creative discourse behind the scenes between the architect or client on the one hand and the model-maker as the portraitist of the idea on the other. In the words of the architect and theorist Gänshirt, »Model-making is thinking with your hands; it almost amounts to building«.[70] The model, as a sculptural embodiment of the design idea, then enters the spotlight of a public discussion of the idea which would not be possible without the existence of the model. It is the observer who determines the details and finer points of the design on which to focus. Like the lens of a camera, the observer approaches or retreats, circles the model or allows his gaze to rove over and through it. The range of impressions that reaches the observer's eye resembles the panning of a camera after a film sequence »which, in the case of architecture, continues after a change of position«.[71] Rudolf Arnheim coined the term »consecutive observation« for the visual perception of architecture in its actual size and explained that it was a consequence of the »imbalance between the size of human beings and their buildings«.[72] As early as the nineteenth century, Hermann Maertens had derived his »optical scale«[73] based on the human

---

70 Gänshirt (see note 3).
71 Vana (see note 34), p. 40.
72 Rudolf Arnheim, Die Dynamik der architektonischen Form, Cologne 1980, p. 133.

perceptive faculties. According to Vana, Maertens' main concern was to »eliminate inaccuracies from the perception of architectural compositions«. Accordingly, »the model, too, which takes the distance of the observer into account, should be free from allusions and ambiguities«.[74] This visual aspect was also a central issue in Alberti's remarks on the purpose of models.

What was new was the omission of detail to achieve this purpose. The same device accounted for the »modernism of the *Metropolis* sets«. Although not mandatory, this strategy expressed itself as the »radicalisation of the aesthetic intention«[75] which found an echo in avant-garde architecture. In a sense, Modernist architecture was a mirror-image magnification of the model. For example, it is not columns or supports that constitute the crucial features of an architectural model; rather, the art lies in using material means to express floating and load-bearing elements, lightness and heaviness. This may be why the charm – or, in Gänshirt's words, the inherent magic – of a good architectural model lies in simplification. Simplification and deceleration are mutually interdependent, and both result in pragmatic solutions.

The pragmatism lies in the value of the architectural model itself. By scaling down the architecture to the proportions of a doll's house, the architect is magnified to the size of a giant relative to his own creation. At the same time, the model provides the only moment when the architect can tower over his work, as it were, and view it like a Gulliver in the Lilliputian world of his own design adventures. It is this inversion of size relationships that is a necessary prerequisite for democratic discussion which allows for evaluation, judgment and decision-making before the scale model is supplanted by the full-scale building in real life. Hiesmayr summarises this state of affairs as follows: »Thrown back upon our bodily nature, we live through the relationship of the body to the model, and from this we derive the model's usefulness.«[76] This, perhaps, is the reason why the shortest route to comprehending the nature of the Renaissance model leads through reflection on the design leitmotifs of Modernism.

City model of Mekka/Saudi-Arabia
Scale: 1:500
Photo: Peter Mallauschek, Stuttgart

74 Vana (see note 34), p. 69.
75 Ibid.
76 Ernst Hiesmayr (see note 64).

Modellbau Milde – Tilman Burgert
Berlin

Persian Gulf Center Shiraz
Presentation model, 2005
Architect: von Gerkan, Marg und Partner
Scale: 1:500
Material: Pear wood and acrylic glass,
etched nickel silver sheets
Photo: Tilman Burgert

www.modellbau-milde.de

Modellbau Milde was founded in Berlin in 1973. From the outset, the number one priority in this company rich in tradition was quality, along with the aim to produce models that convey an initial impression of a design idea and activate a feeling for the proportions. Part of this is the realisation that wood is still the most suitable material for stimulating contemplation and imagination. Moreover, model-makers know that it very often has observers itching to touch the model in order to obtain a material response, a haptic confirmation of what they are seeing. Consequently, Modellbau Milde relies almost exclusively on the expressive power of the raw material used. This applies not only to wood. For the other characteristic feature of this high-tech company, whose broad spectrum ranges from making industrial and technical cast models via design right through to the automotive sector, is its formal vocabulary. The credo for architectural models by Modellbau Milde (Prop.: Tilman Burgert) could be »Material and Form«. From rendering to finished models in a wide range of scales, scale representations are distinguished by a very high degree of precision. The visual rendering technique enables the customer to alter material, colourings and design details before Modellbau Milde begins constructing the model. As with a real building, clients are kept informed of the intermediate stages of the construction process. E-mailed digital photos enable the client to be, as it were, the site supervisor of events on the workbench.

Continuous exposure to new requirements has led to the discovery of new materials and processing methods and, as a result, to amazing combinations of materials, including plastic metals and softly translucent concrete. But this is only the beginning. The dream extends beyond this, to freely mouldable, wafer-thin luminous filaments, noiseless miniature drive mechanisms and materials that can be moulded into various programmed shapes at the touch of a button.

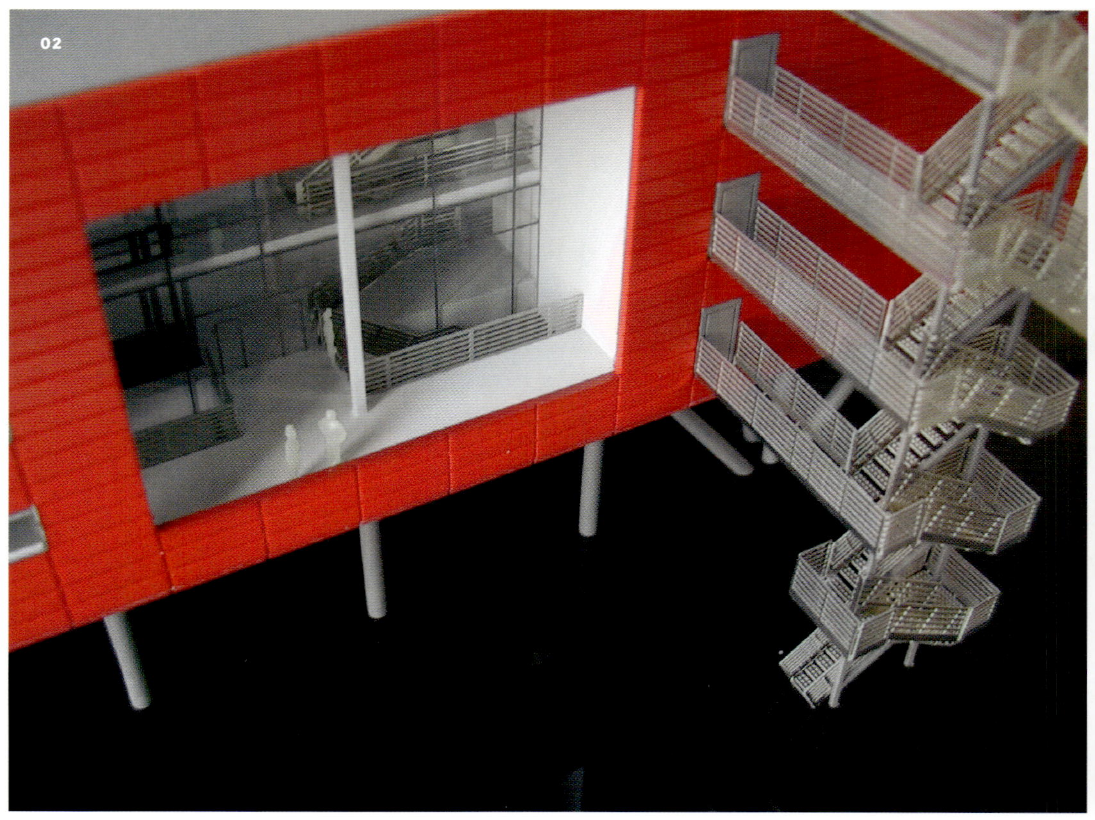

01 / 02 / 03 / 04

Info Box, Leipziger Platz, Berlin
Presentation model, 2003
Architect: Schneider und Schumacher
Scale: 1:200
Material: Polystyrene, acrylic glass, etched nickel silver
Photos: Tilman Burgert

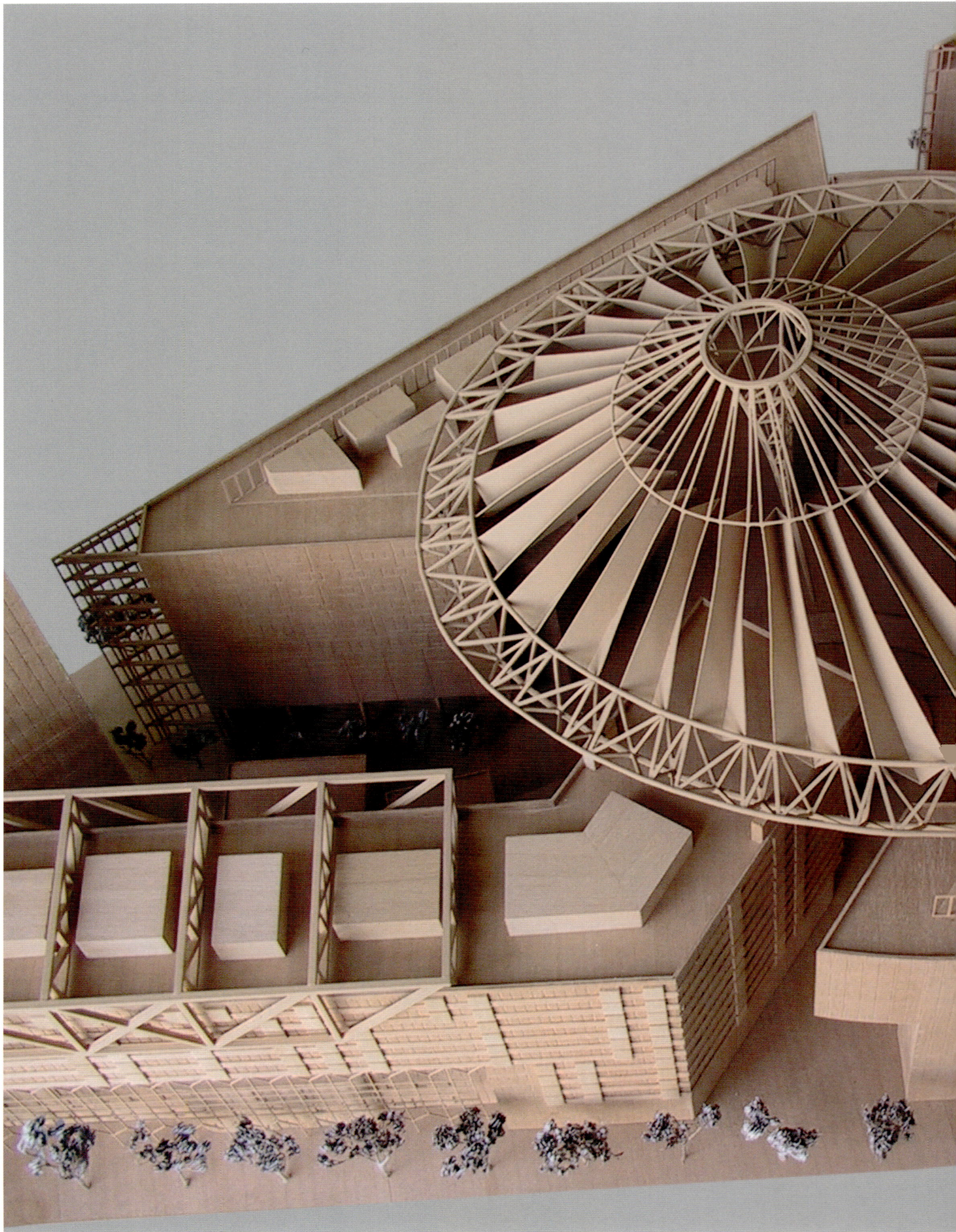

SONY Center, Berlin
Presentation model, 2003
Architect: Helmut Jahn
Material: Pear wood
Photo: Tilman Burgert

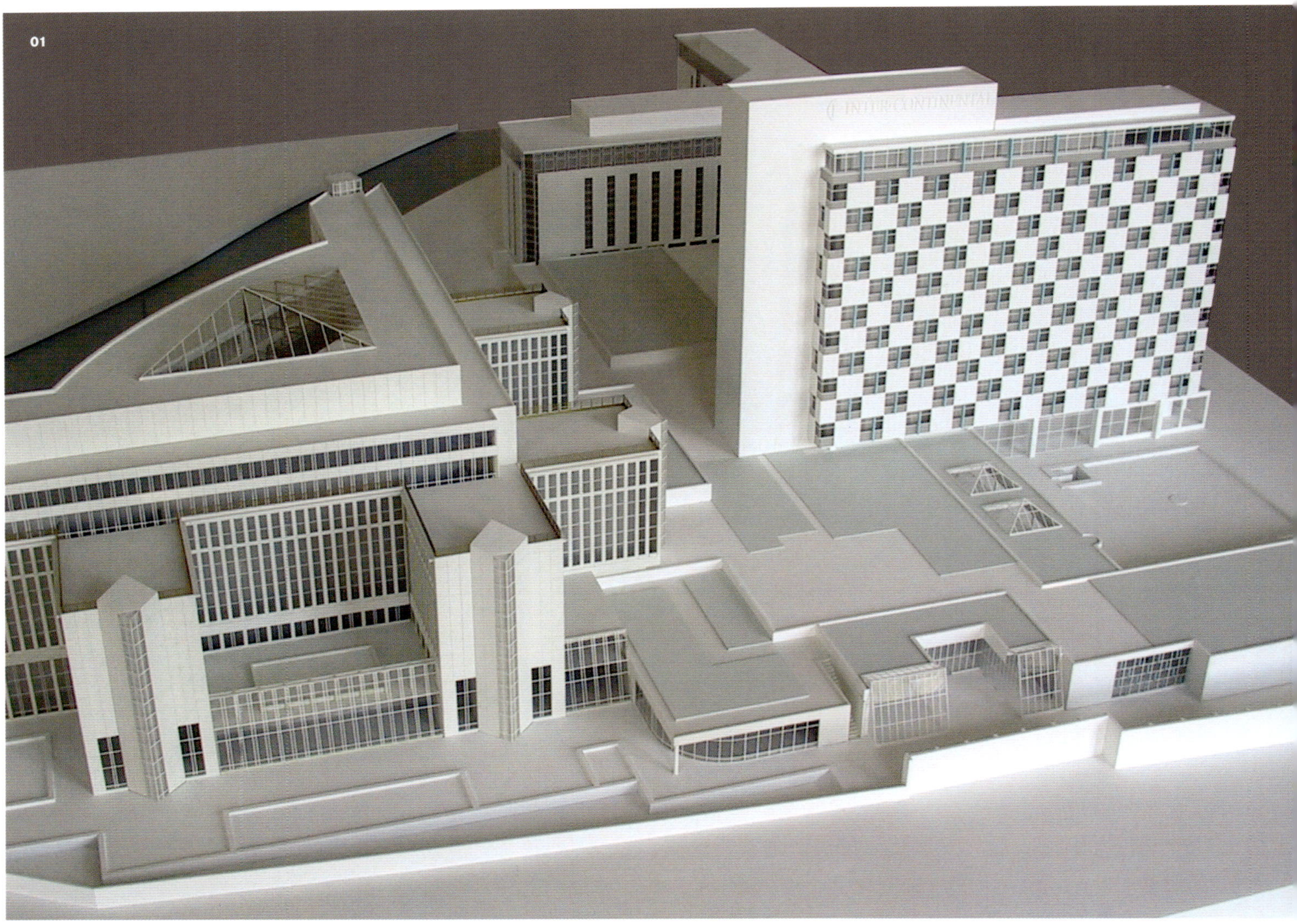

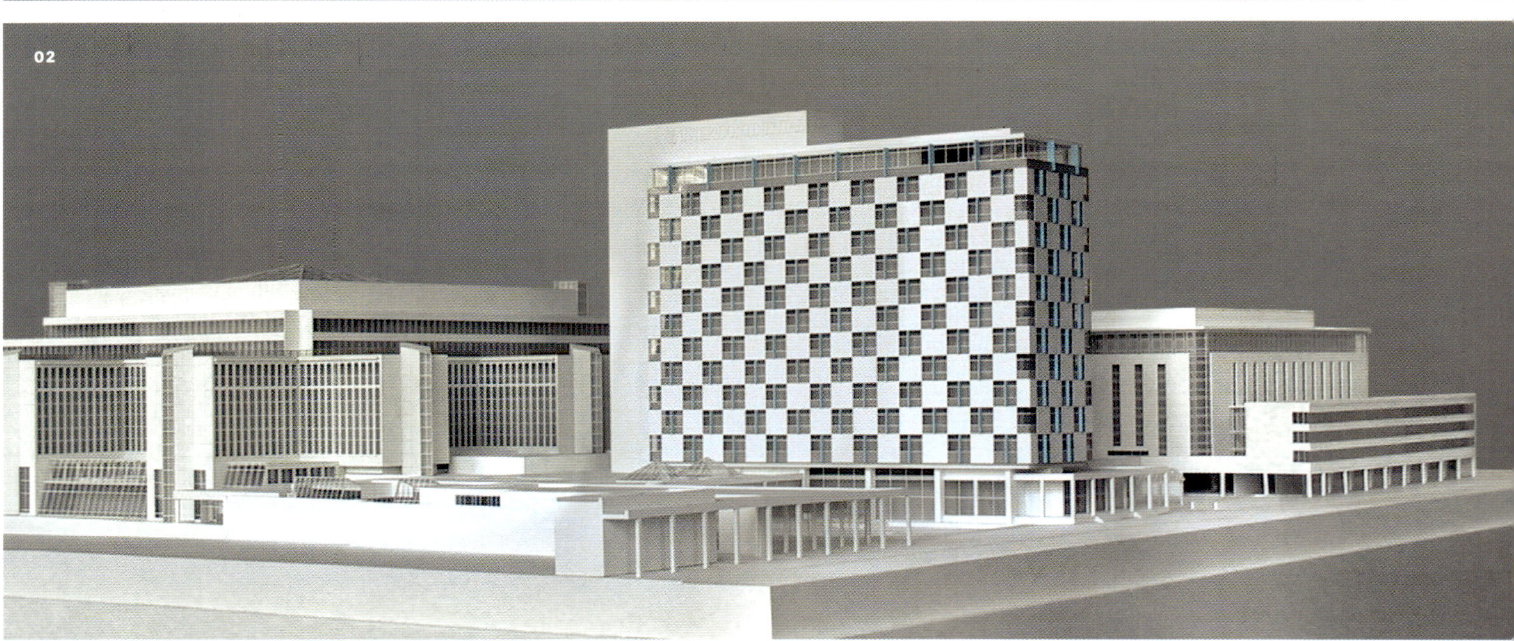

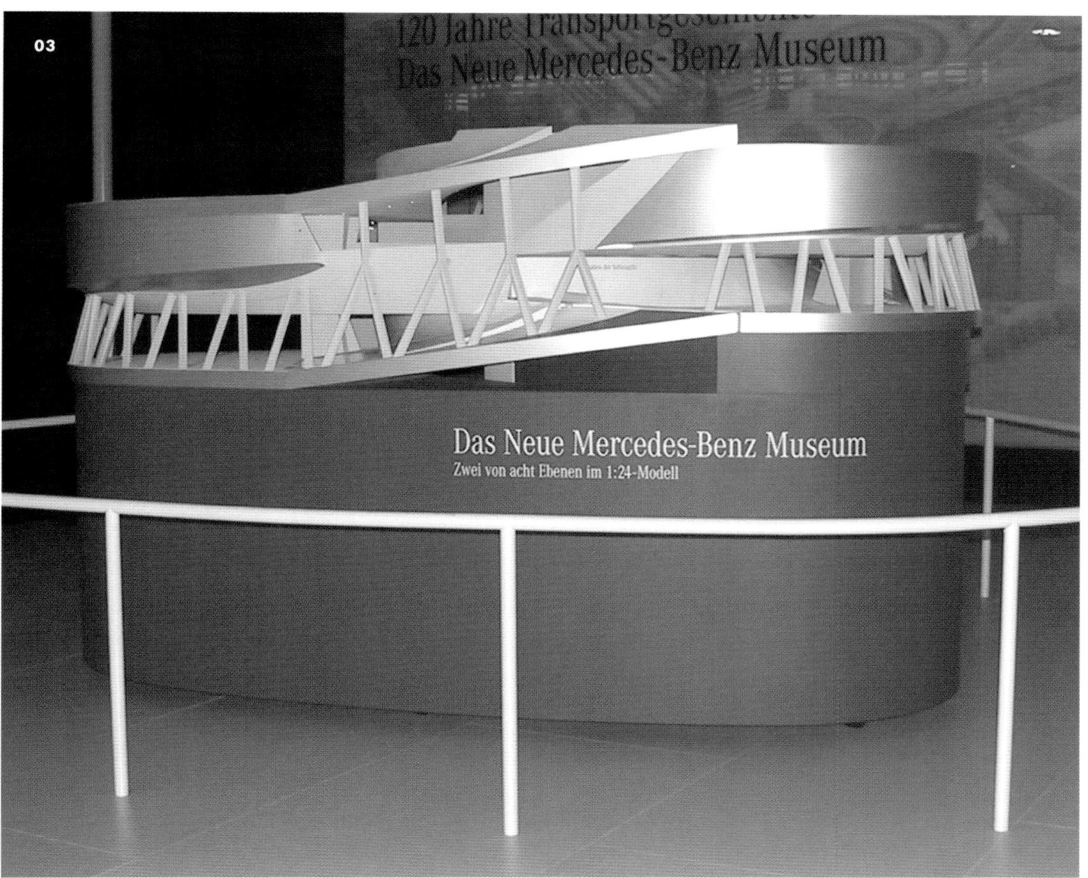

Hotel Interconti, Berlin
Presentation model, 2003
Scale: 1:200
Material: Acrylic glass, polystyrene
Photos: Tilman Burgert

03

Mercedes-Benz Museum, Stuttgart
Presentation model, 2003
Architect: UN Studio
Client: DaimlerChrysler Immobilien GmbH
Scale: 1:24
Material: Fibre optic lighting, cold cathode lamps,
polystyrene
Photo: Tilman Burgert

04

Bread & Butter Fashion Show, Berlin,
with coloured illumination
Presentation model, 2005
Scale: 1:50
Material: Polystyrene, acrylic glass
Photo: Tilman Burgert

Abu Dhabi City
Illuminated competition model, 2005
Architect: Neumann Gusenburger Architekten
Scale: 1:5,000
Material: Acrylic glass, polystyrene
Photo: Tilman Burgert

01

AREVA
02

01 ....
Warehouse on the Spree by Oberbaumbrücke, Berlin
Presentation model, 2000
Architect: Architekturbüro Reinhard Müller
Scale: 1:200
Material: Acrylic glass, polystyrene
Photo: Tilman Burgert

02 ....
Areva Transformer Station
Presentation model, 2005
Scale: 1:50
Material: Acrylic glass, polystyrene
Photo: Tilman Burgert

03 ....
Model for the film *Die armen Hunde* (Poor Dogs)
Feierabendhaus building, Hürth
Model intended for deliberate destruction
by water penetrating through panes.
Client: EYE Warning Filmproduktion GbR;
Dominik & Ben Reding
Scale: 1:100
Material: Polystyrene, acrylic glass with
deliberate cracks
Photo: Tilman Burgert

04 ....
Entrance Building to
Krumme Lanke U-Bahn Station, Berlin
Architect: Alfred Grenander, 1929
Client: Deutsches Technikmuseum Berlin
Scale: 1:100
Material: Acrylic glass, polystyrene, lighting technology
Photo: Tilman Burgert

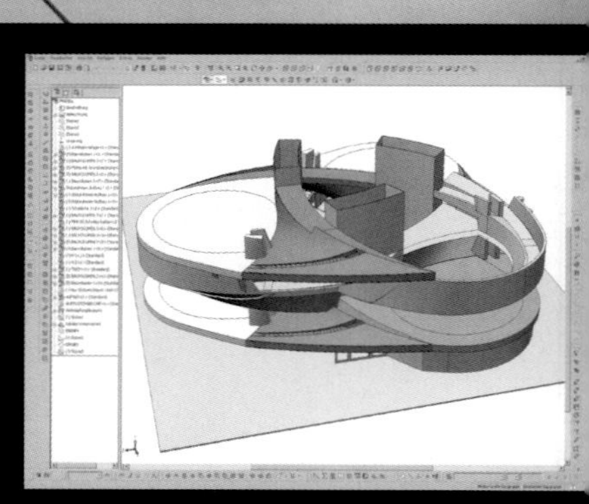

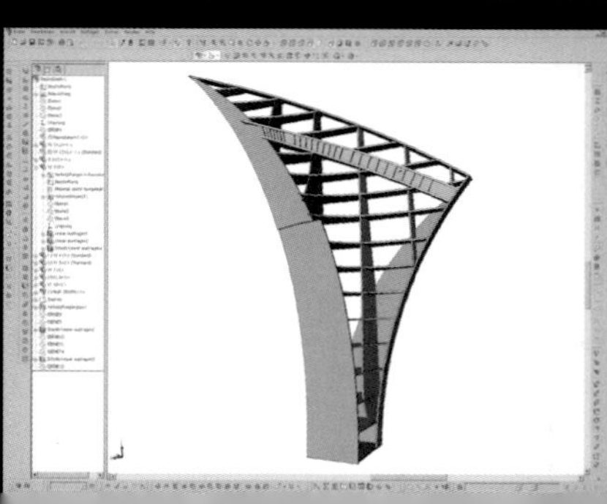

01

Model Construction Works, Mercedes-Benz Museum
in Stuttgart, 2003
Checking the light situation
(incidence of daylight and artificial light).

02

Model Construction Works, Mercedes-Benz Museum
in Stuttgart, 2003
Illuminated ceiling from the model, lit by cold cathode
lamps; on the right, virtual volume constructions
on a scale of 1:24.

03/04

Model Construction Works, Mercedes-Benz Museum
in Stuttgart, 2003
Assembly: In order to replicate the free forms specified
by the architect, the model maker must find his or her
own solution. In this case, the free form is constructed
with the help of formers.

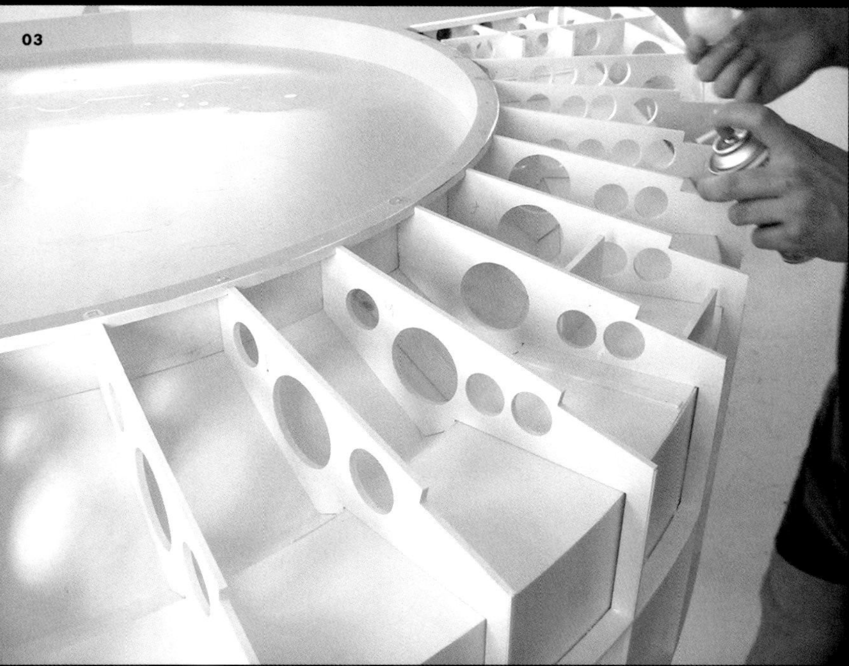

Dieter Cöllen

Cologne

www.coellen-cork.com

Dieter Cöllen has been making architectural models since the early 1980s. His core concern is to try to understand an architect's design from the initial idea sketched on a paper tablecloth over lunch and, by doing so, in effect to adopt it as his own. In this way Cöllen, as it were in the capacity of first executive assistant to the architect, creates an interpretation of the design and in his model builds the first version of the planned architecture. His keen sense of the design's distinctive language determines the choice of material and technical execution. Like an artist in search of the right material for a work of art, Cöllen is always on the lookout for new materials to lend expression to the architect's idea and the planned work of architecture. Research, studies of historic buildings and, not least, his experience in building architectural models have enabled Cöllen to uncover the closely guarded secrets of traditional phelloplastics (modelling in cork), a technique he has used and refined to high technical and artistic standards. Due to its colouring and surface structure, this gnarled natural material is reserved for depicting the present state of historic buildings from antiquity to the Middle Ages.

The visual idiosyncrasy of the surface structure of cork compels a reduction to buildings' prominent stylistic elements; the originality of the reproduction bears the model-maker's personal handwriting. This purist approach is combined with meticulous preparatory work that involves analysing old engravings, visiting original locations and cooperating with archaeologists and architectural historians. The cork models are developed on the basis of up-to-date research and findings. His approach to them also informs Cöllen's architectural models of modern buildings.

Tivoli Temple
Model: Dieter Cöllen
Scale: 1:33
Material: Cork
Collection of Prof. O. M. Ungers, Cologne
Photo: Rainer Mader

01

02

03

01

Temple of Poseidon, Paestum 450 BC
Model: Dieter Cöllen
Scale: 1:50
Material: Cork
Photo: Rainer Mader

02

Valentré Bridge, Cahors
Model: Dieter Cöllen
Scale: 1:100
Material: Cork
Photo: Rainer Mader

03

Arch of Drusus, Rome
Model: Dieter Cöllen
Scale: 1:33
Material: Cork
Collection of Prof. O. M. Ungers, Cologne
Photo: Rainer Mader

04

Temple of Castor and Pollux, Sparta
Model: Dieter Cöllen
Scale: 1:20
Material: Cork
Photo: Holger Knauf

01
02

03

04

01

Differentials
Architect: Thomas van den Valentyn
Model: Dieter Cöllen with Torsten Fiedler
Scale: 1:500
Material: Satinised perspex
Photo: Rainer Mader

02

Office/Interior
Architect: Erlen + Partner
Model: Dieter Cöllen with Torsten Fiedler
Scale: 1:100
Material: Wood, plastic
Photo: Holger Knauf

03

Compass Needle, Groningen
Architect: Josef Paul Kleihues
Model: Dieter Cöllen with Torsten Fiedler
Scale: 1:200
Material: Aluminium, brass
Photo: Rainer Mader

04

Metzler and LHB Bank Tower, Frankfurt am Main, 2001
Architect: Gatermann + Schossig
Model: Dieter Cöllen with Torsten Fiedler
Scale: 1:500
Material: Perspex
Photo: Rainer Mader

01/02/03 ....

Helfmann Park Eschborn
Architect: RKW Düsseldorf
Model: Dieter Cöllen with Torsten Fiedler
Scale: 1:500
Material: Perspex, polysterene
Photos: Holger Knauf

Robert Endres
Bamberg

www.robert-endres.de

Robert Endres focuses mainly on models of entire townscapes. In terms of content this means reconstructing historical states, either for museums and documentations of various kinds or to serve as a basis for conservation work. Models of this type are always preceded by detailed archive research. This involves analysing historical images or descriptions of a house, a street, etc., from an assortment of documents depending on subject and era. Where the scaled-down version renders existing architectures tangible, the aim is to contrast their original appearance as recreated in the model with the current situation. An architectural model is built on the basis of drawings, either existing drawings or dimensioned drawings produced in-house. Work on models of districts or whole cities and on dimensioned drawings requires close observation and an in-depth study of all manner of historical sources that may lie buried in archives or in the buildings themselves. The area model of the Berlin Wall section between the boroughs of Mitte and Wedding is an example of a model produced in this way. Created for the Berlin Wall Documentation Center, it shows the situation in 1965.

The houses with bricked-up windows on the Bernauer Strasse border between East and West Berlin were demolished soon after 1965; the tenements were cleared when parts of the Wedding district were razed and redeveloped in the 1970s; the Church of Reconciliation was dynamited in 1985. Photos from records of the Wedding redevelopment zone prior to demolition were the principal sources for this model. The architectural model thus records and reconstructs a historical situation. Made for conservation purposes, however, it not only shows the past, but impacts on the present. Only a few distinctive façade elements are included, and the materials employed are very straightforward. Chipboard and cardboard or corrugated board (also used for the unrealised *Unter den Mühlen* model produced for a competition for a building on the Regnitz peninsula in Bamberg) are not only low-cost but, in the case of the Berlin Wall model, in their raw state reflect the morbid and desolate atmosphere of the prohibited zone between East and West.

Model of the Berlin Wall in 1965
Ackerstrasse from the north.
At the top edge of the picture is the intersection with Bernauer Strasse. Wall on Bernauer Strasse with border posts in Sophienfriedhof cemetery.
Only the postwar buildings and the Lazarus Hospital (top right corner of the picture) still exist.
Research collaborator: Rainer Just
Completed: 1995/98

01

Model of the Berlin Wall in 1965
Section at Hussitenstrasse 59/58 (no longer existent);
area model, historical state
Client: Evangelische Versöhnungsgemeinde, Berlin;
Verein Berliner Mauer e. V., Berlin
Scale: 1:500
Material: Chipboard, cardboard
Completed: 1995 (model section shown)

02

Model of the Berlin Wall in 1965
Hussitenstrasse 71, 70, 69
(No. 71 no longer exists)
Completed: 1995

03

Model of the Berlin Wall in 1965
Bernauer Strasse between Strelitzer Strasse
and the Reconciliation Church.
View of bricked-up houses on the border
(in the foreground West Berlin, in the
 background East Berlin).
None of the buildings shown here survive.
Research collaborators: Maria Nooke, Rainer Just
Completed: 1998

01 
02

03
Ackerstraße

01

Model of the Berlin Wall in 1965
Bernauer Strasse, looking southwest from Ruppiner
Strasse. On the left, bricked-up houses along the border,
on the right the (West Berlin) borough of Wedding.
Most of the buildings shown here no longer exist.
Research collaborators: Maria Nooke, Rainer Just
Completed: 2002

02

Model of the Berlin Wall in 1965
Hussitenstrasse 64-59. Only the Ernst Reuter estate
(in the background, 1954) still exists.
Completed: 1995

03

Model of the Berlin Wall in 1965
Corner of Ackerstrasse and Feldstrasse.
Ernst Reuter estate in the centre of the picture.
Completed: 1995

04

Bernauer Strasse 83-80 (West Berlin), 1965
Photographic record commissioned by
the Arbeitsgruppe für Stadtplanung (AGS)
Landesarchiv, Berlin

05

Bernauer Strasse 89-87 (West Berlin), 1965
Photographic record commissioned by
the Arbeitsgruppe für Stadtplanung (AGS)
Landesarchiv, Berlin

06

Bernauer Strasse 16 / 15, 1965
Bricked-up houses on the border
Photographic record commissioned by
the Arbeitsgruppe für Stadtplanung (AGS)
Landesarchiv, Berlin

03

01/02/03

Untere Mühlen, Bamberg
Operational model
Architect: Jürgen Rudroff Architekturbüro, Bamberg
Client: Dipl.-Ing. E. O. Kanold, Berlin
Existing: Solid beech, birch plywood, mirror foil
Plan: Corrugated board
Scale: 1:100
Completed: 2000
Photos: Robert Endres
The plan is shown as a simple mass model
without detailing, the incorporated ruin with windows
and cornices.

04

Untere Mühlen, Bamberg
View looking downstream from Bischofsmühlbrücke
bridge (2000).
Photo: Robert Endres

05

Untere Mühlen, Bamberg
Ruins of Sterzersmühle mill (2000).
Detail matches model photo 01 on this page.
Photo: Robert Endres

04

05

Stephan Fleig and Andreas Fofana
Karlsruhe

www.werk-plan.de

Werkplan was founded in 1999, though the collaboration between the company's two proprietors, Stephan Fleig and Andreas Fofana, dates back to the mid-1990s. Both men studied architecture, but their qualifications are diametrically opposed. While Fleig earned his laurels in the field of archaeology and conservation of historic buildings, Fofana developed his career profile with a supplementary apprenticeship as a cabinetmaker and by working as a woodworker in the planning and execution of furniture and interior design projects. These different career paths not only give the company two main pillars, furniture-making and architectural model-making, but also lead to unique overlaps in their style as craftsmen. This is manifested in the demonstration models themselves, in the range of models and in their execution. In terms of range, Werkplan make everything from working models that accompany designs to competition models.

Their unique quality lies in their self-conception as planners and craftsmen. Their architectural training enables them to grasp a design idea or understand an ancient site. Moreover, they can look back on twenty years' experience of model-making, of translating design ideas into a characteristic model-making language so as to communicate the statement made by the architecture.

The way the two men's career profiles interact is manifested clearly in the case of reconstruction models, where the aim is to resurrect a past situation in a model on the basis of research into architectural history and archaeology. Each task in this category calls for its own mode of translation into model form, both in terms of the level of abstraction or detail and of the materials used, the colouring and scale. Regardless of material, which is usually pear wood, their historical models also evince that reduction to the salient elements of the architectural design that is responsible for the clarity of those of modern buildings. In each case, differences in the architecture are highlighted by the use of contrasting materials. These, however, harmonise in such a way that the model itself is a small sculpture, a unique piece, like the model of the school in Bühl.

Hattusa
Location: Kunsthalle Bonn, 2002
Client: Kunst- und Ausstellungshalle
der Bundesrepublik Deutschland, Bonn
Scale: 1:500
Material: Pear woods, MDF
Photo: Werkplan

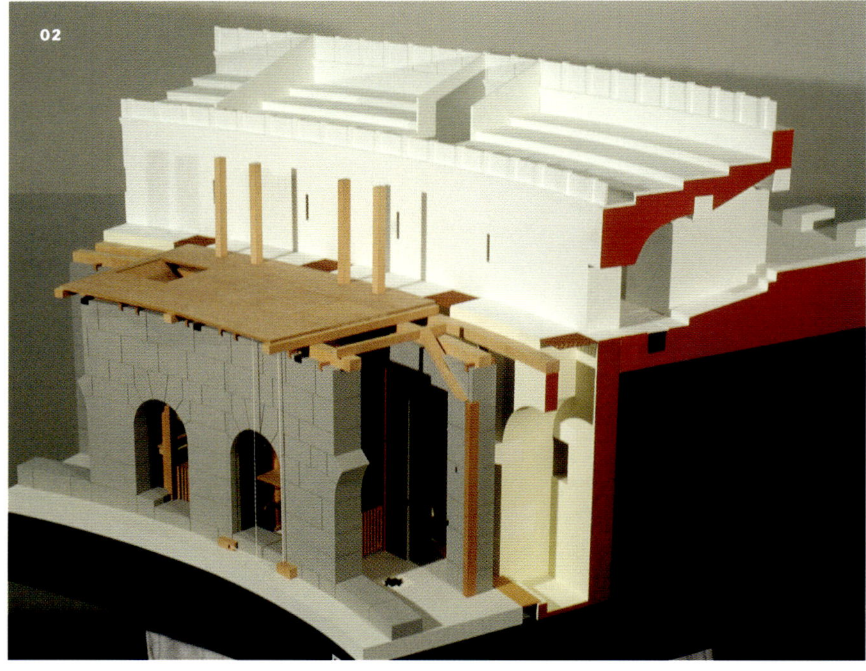

01 / 02 / 03

Colosseum, Rome, lifts
SANGUE E ARENA exhibition, 2001
Client: Soprintendenza Archeologica di Roma
Scale: 1:50
Material: Pear wood, MDF
Photos: Werkplan

04 / 05

Northern Fortifications, Selinunte, Sicily, c. 400 BC
1990
Client: DAI Rome
for Selinunte Archaeological Museum
Scale: 1:200
Material: Pear wood, MDF
Photos: Werkplan

01

02

03

04

05

06

01/02

Model of the town of Sama'al (Zincirli) in the border
region between Turkey and Syria, c. 8th century BC
Reconstruction by the archaeologist and architectural
historian Robert Koldewey, 1999
Client: Reiss-Museum Mannheim
Scale: 1:500
Material: Polystyrene
Photos: Werkplan

03/04

Model of the Babylonian royal city of Uruk,
Iraq, 5th millennium BC
1999
Client: Reiss-Museum Mannheim
Scale: 1:500
Material: Polystyrene
Photos: Werkplan

05/06

Castel del Monte, Apulia, Italy
Client: Württembergisches Landesmuseum,
Stuttgart, 2000
Scale: 1:50
Material: Pear wood, MDF
Photos: Werkplan

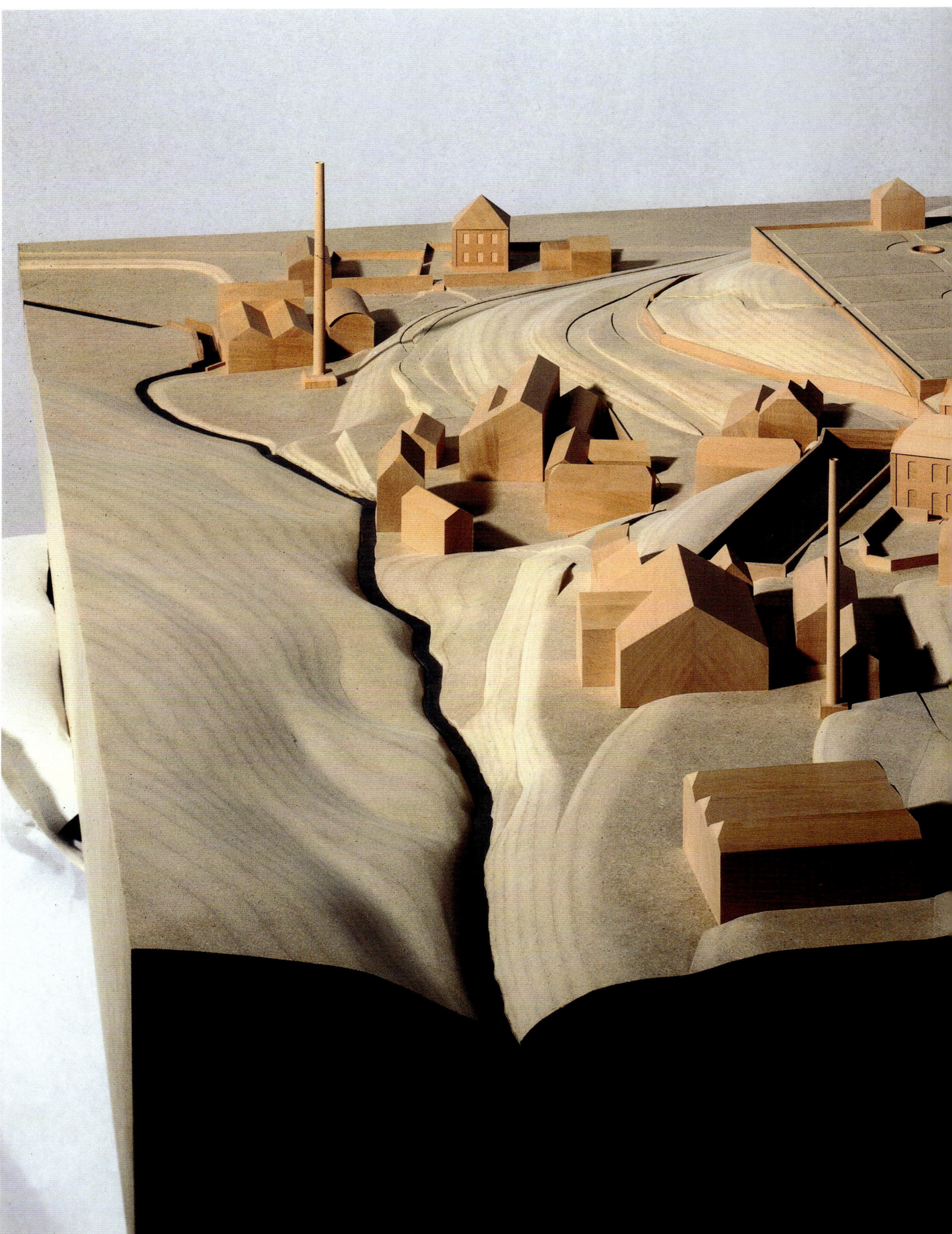

Ironworks in Weilerbach, District of Bitburg, 1779-1914
Client: Schloss Weilerbach-Gesellschaft, Bitburg
1998
Scale: 1:333
Material: Pear wood, MDF
Photo: Werkplan

03

01 / 02 / 03

01 / 02 / 03 ....

King's Throne, Rhens (1398)
Der Griff nach der Krone (Reaching for the Crown)
exhibition, 2000
Client: Oberfinanzdirektion Karlsruhe,
Abteilung Staatliche Schlösser und Gärten,
Baden-Württemberg
Scale: 1:25
Material: MDF, casting resin, rigid polyurethane foam
Photos: Werkplan

01

01

School and Library, Bühl
Competition
Architect: AGP Architekten
Scale: 1:500
Material: Pear wood, acrylic glass, aluminium
Photo: Werkplan

02/03

Youth Centre in Frankfurt, 2004,
Competition
Architect: Kränzle + Fischer-Wasels
Scale: 1:200
Material: Wenge
Photos: Thilo Mechau

02

03

Bernd Grimm

Cologne

www.plastermodel.com

Bernd Grimm has worked with alabaster plaster for twenty years. A specialist in high-quality architectural models, he uses a material that goes back to ancient times. His three-dimensional miniatures made of alabaster plaster have an air of immortality. At the same time, this bright, timeless material is suitable for representing both historical and modern architectures. Grimm's models are objects in their own right. Fashioned from a material rarely seen in competitions, they stand out on account of their superb quality. The neutral-toned elegance of alabaster plaster steers the eye of the beholder to the representation of the planned reality. Because of its material properties, plaster can achieve results that make a strong impact yet seem unobtrusive. For modern projects, Grimm also builds models up to a scale of 1:10 in wood or board.

Grimm's speciality is constructing replicas of historic architectures whose sculptural character has secured them a place in exhibitions and museums. Constructing miniature editions of buildings, interiors, rural and urban architectures in plaster requires a close study of historical papers on architecture as well as building surveys, plans, sketches and photographs. The next step is to decide the scale and form of representation, that is, whether an exterior view or a section is to be produced.

In addition to an in-depth knowledge of architecture and construction theory, this kind of model-making also involves manual work with tools that are often specially made by the artists himself. A strong sense of timing is needed to take advantage of the material's flowability so that it can subsequently be worked with sandpaper and a scribing iron. Errors have serious consequences because they cause delays. After a lengthy period of work, a sculptural piece of architecture emerges that is as unique as a Greek statue – witnessing techniques in which only a few are proficient and which require a great deal of experience. Grimm accordingly sees his work as »intellectual craftsmanship«. His models are intermediaries between past and present.

Tempietto, S. Pietro in Montorio 1502, Rome
Architect: Donato Bramante
Scale: 1:15
Material: Alabaster plaster
Collection of Prof. O. M. Ungers, Cologne
Photo: Jan Kraege, Cologne

01

Detailed view of the Tempietto
Photo: Jan Kraege, Cologne

02

Detailed drawing of the Tempietto

03

Sketch for model design

04

Basis for work: Paul Letarouilly,
Édifices de Rome Moderne, Paris 1856

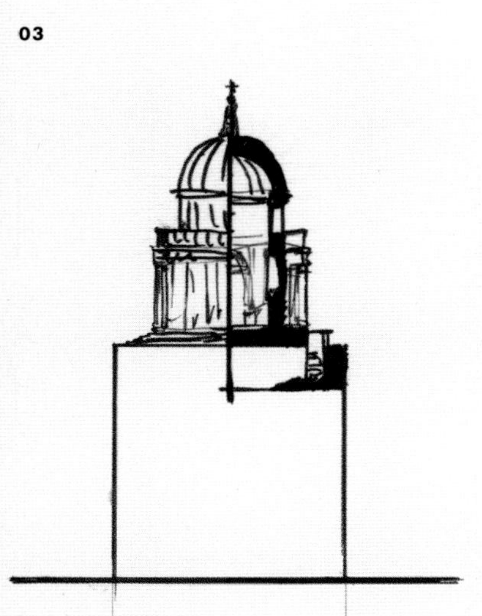

Situations-Plan der Grossherzoglichen Residenz Stadt Karlsruhe.

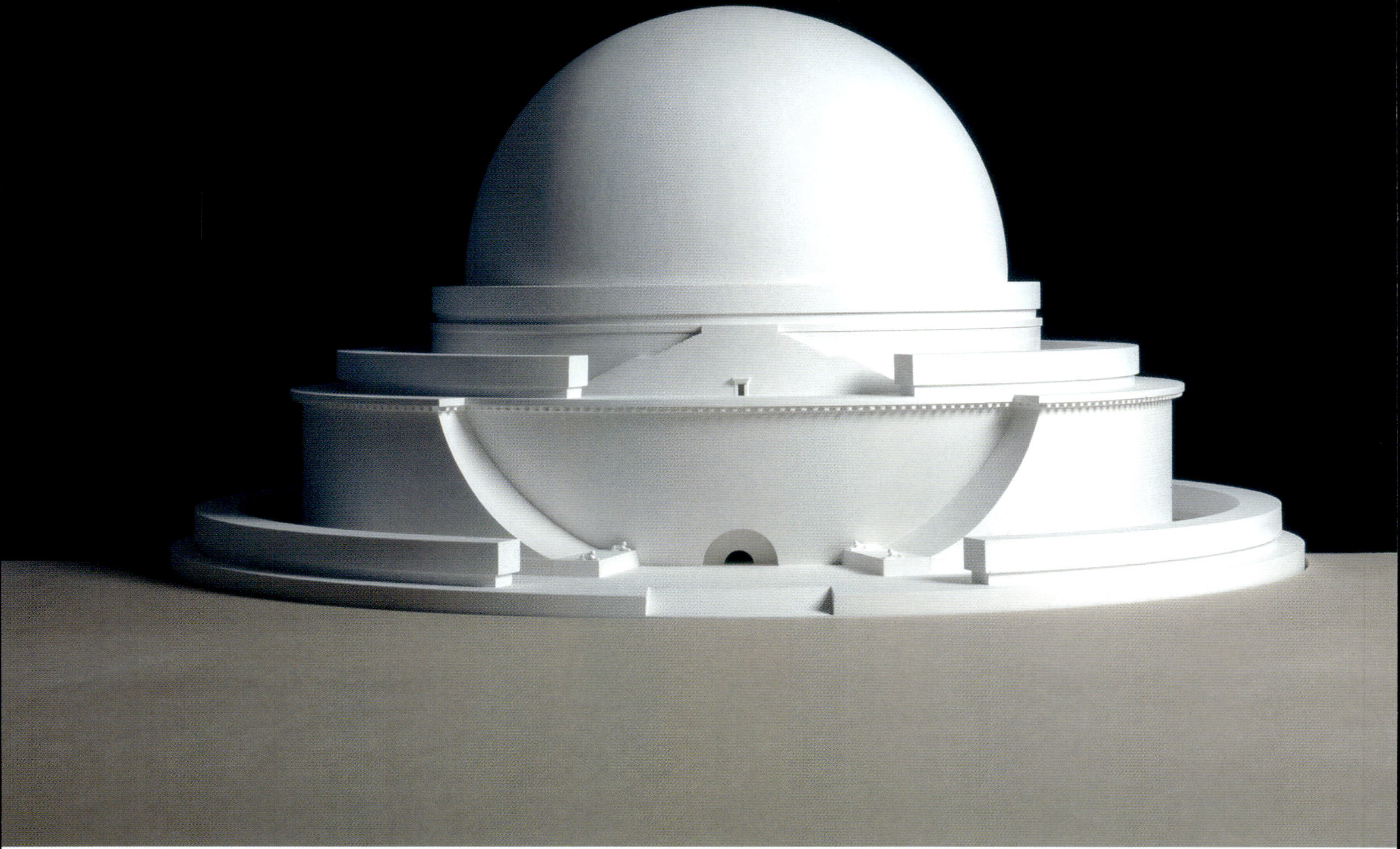

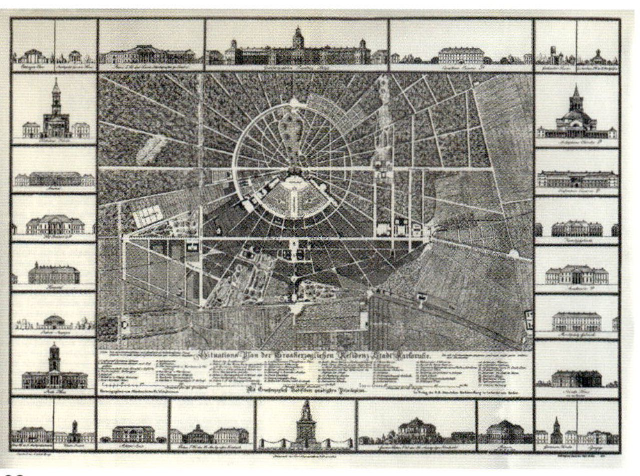

02

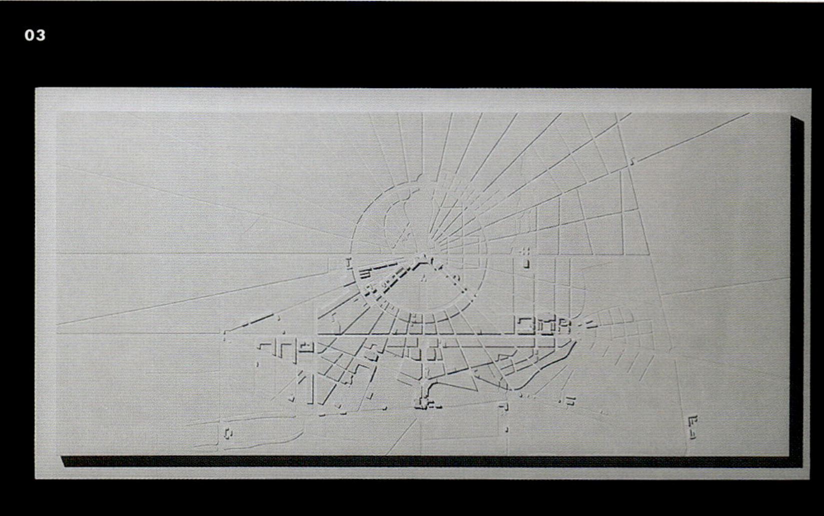

03

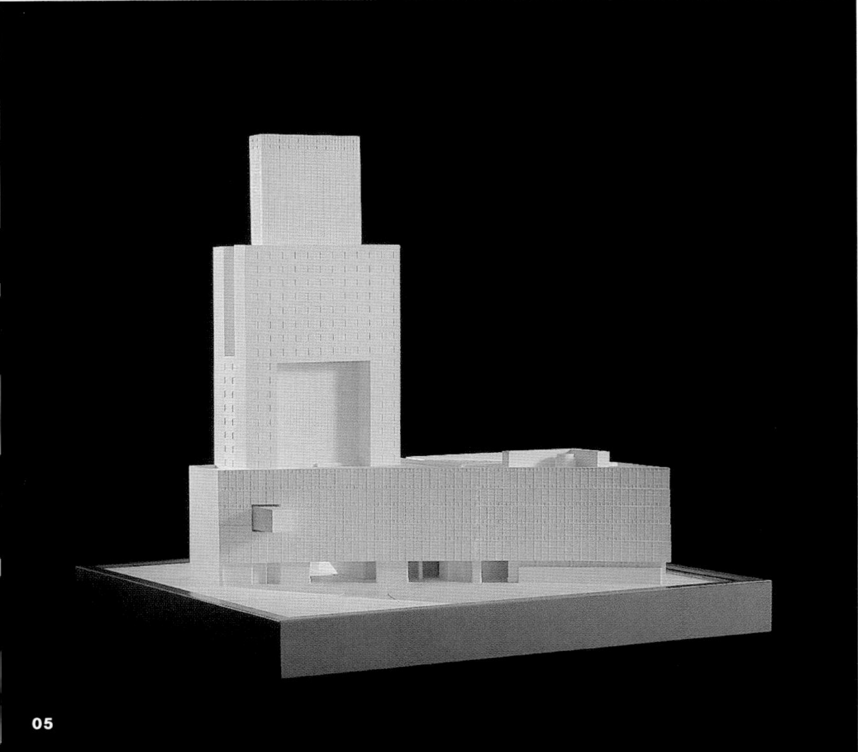

01

Newton's Cenotaph, 1784
Architect: Etienne Louis Boulée
Scale: 1:400
Material: Alabaster plaster
Collection of Prof. O. M. Ungers, Cologne
Photo: Jan Kraege, Cologne

02

Karlsruhe c. 1822. Design for urban development
after Friedrich Weinbrenner.

03

Karlsruhe c. 1822
Scale: 1:5.000
Material: Alabaster plaster
Collection of Prof. O. M. Ungers, Cologne
Photo: Bernd Grimm

04

Torhaus (Gatehouse), Frankfurt am Main
Architect: Prof. O. M. Ungers
Photo: Stefan Müller, Berlin

05

Torhaus, Frankfurt am Main
Scale: 1:200
Material: Alabaster plaster
Collection of Prof. O. M. Ungers, Cologne
Photo: Stefan Müller, Berlin

01
02

03

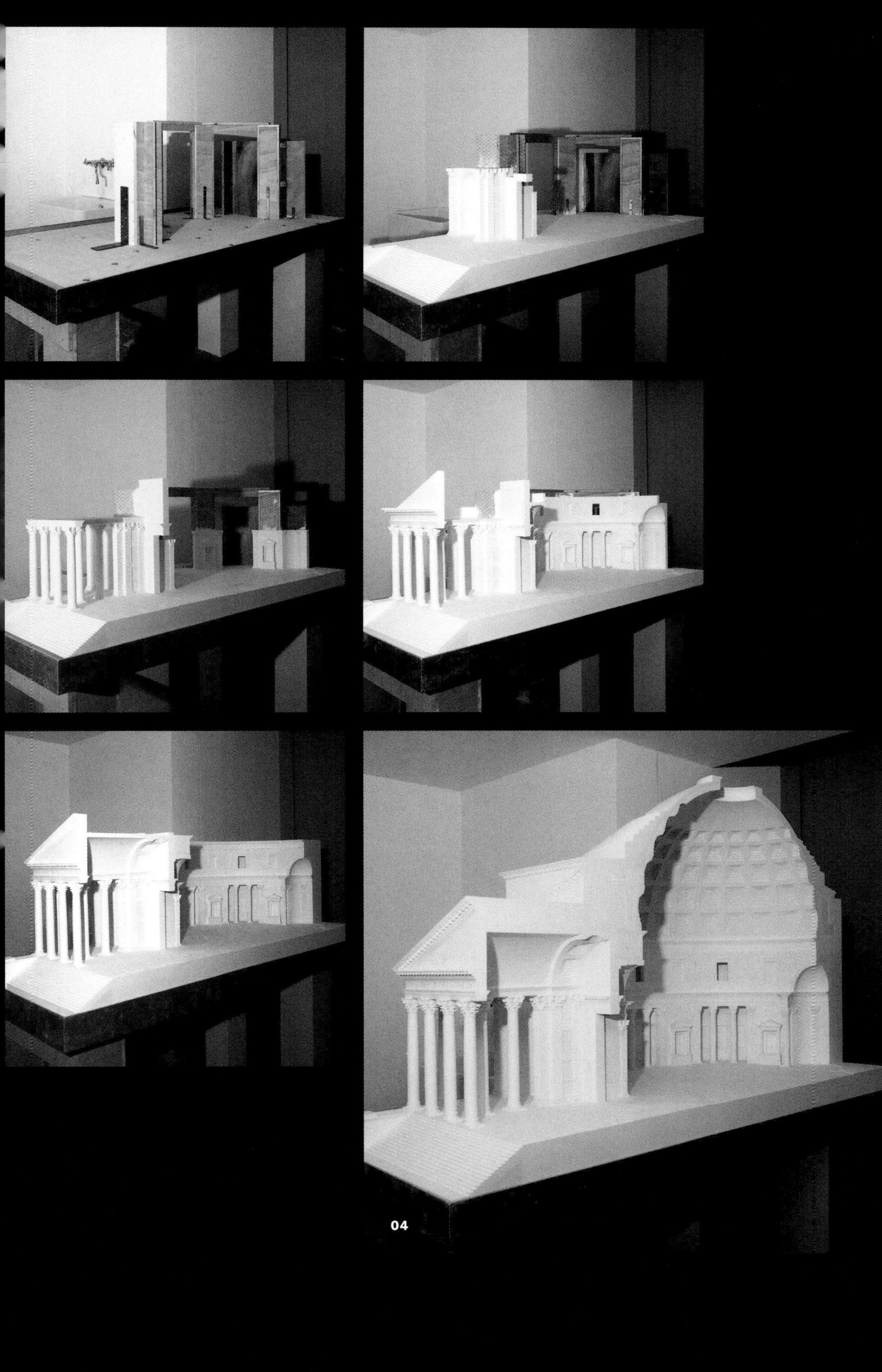

01 ....
Plaster working tool: drawing slide
Photo: Bernd Grimm

02 ....
Plaster working tool: turning slide
Photo: Bernd Grimm

03 ....
Silicon mould – master mould – plaster cast
Photo: Bernd Grimm

04 ....
Constructing a model of the Pantheon in Rome
Scale: 1:50
Photo: Bernd Grimm

Frieder Grüne

Wolfratshausen

www.gruene-modellbau.de

Süddeutscher Verlag Office Building, Munich
Competition model
Architect: Ackermann+Partner
Scale: 1:500
Photo: Ackermann+Partner

When Frieder Grüne, a master foundry-pattern maker, set up in business on his own in 1991, he focused solely on architectural models. His company now has a workforce of eight and covers a range of work, from design to industrial proto-types and wind tunnel models. The firm's expertise in building industrial and de-sign models using silicon moulds for cast models that produce transparent cast parts (including by means of a vacuum casting device) directly benefits their work on architectural models. The specialised materials and production techniques allow realising even unusual forms of representation to scale, e.g. organic archi-tectures. Grüne Modellbau also has technical equipment and software programs with capabilities extending far beyond those used exclusively in architectural model-making.

A further asset is Grüne's sound technical training as a craftsman foundry pat-tern-maker, a trade comparable to that of a machine fitter, in which two skills are paramount – a first-rate ability to read plans and to implement them ac-curately. That may explain the captivatingly cool precision of Grüne Modellbau models. Take, for example, the amazing knife-edge sharpness of the angles in the Südwestmetall model or the detailed execution, despite its small size, of the laboratory building in Trostberg. Here, a model is seen as a perfect technical performance, as a preview of the built architecture, true to the motto that first-rate architecture calls for corresponding quality in the small-scale representa-tion. In the construction segment, the high-tech model-making workshop almost exclusively produces models for competitions. The basis is the sent CAD data, which are specifically modified on the calculator according to the model building in question. These results can be readily exchanged and corrected, if necessary, before the production of parts has begun.

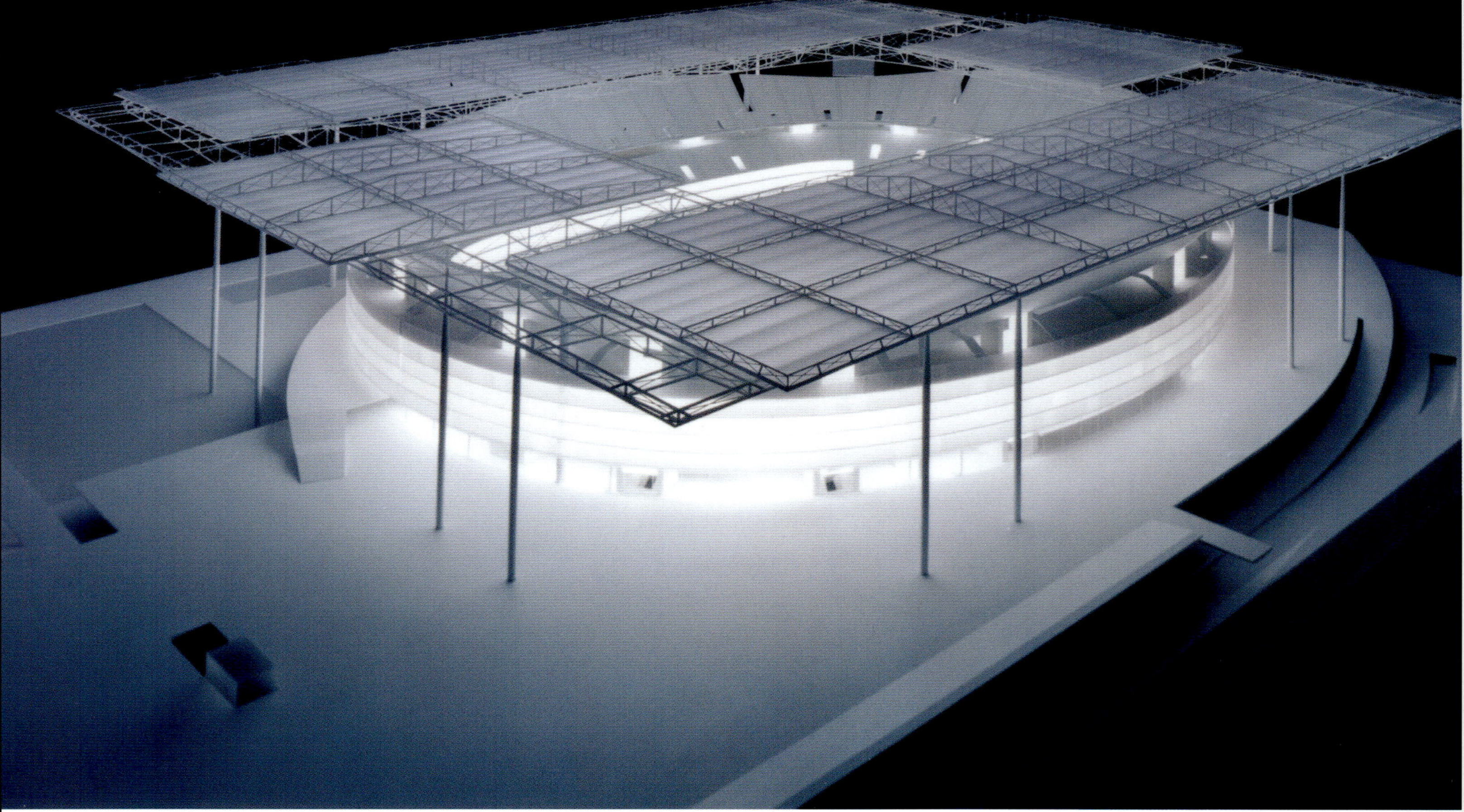

02

01 / 02

FC Bayern Football Arena, 1860, Munich
Competition model
Architect: Auer+Weber+Assoziierte
Scale: 1:500
Photos: Auer+Weber+Assoziierte

03

Bruckmühl High School
Competition model
Architect: Karl + Probst
Scale: 1:500
Photo: Grüne Modellbau

04

Grammar school Bruckmühl
Competition model
Architect: Karl + Probst
Scale: 1:500
Photo: Grüne Modellbau

03

04

01

02

03

01 / 02

Fraunhofer-Gesellschaft, Munich
Presentation model
Architect: Henn Architekten
Scale: 1:200
Photos: Henn Architekten

03 / 04

Südwestmetall, Reutlingen
Presentation model
Architect: Allmann Sattler Wappner Architekten
Scale: 1:100
Photos: Can Cobanli

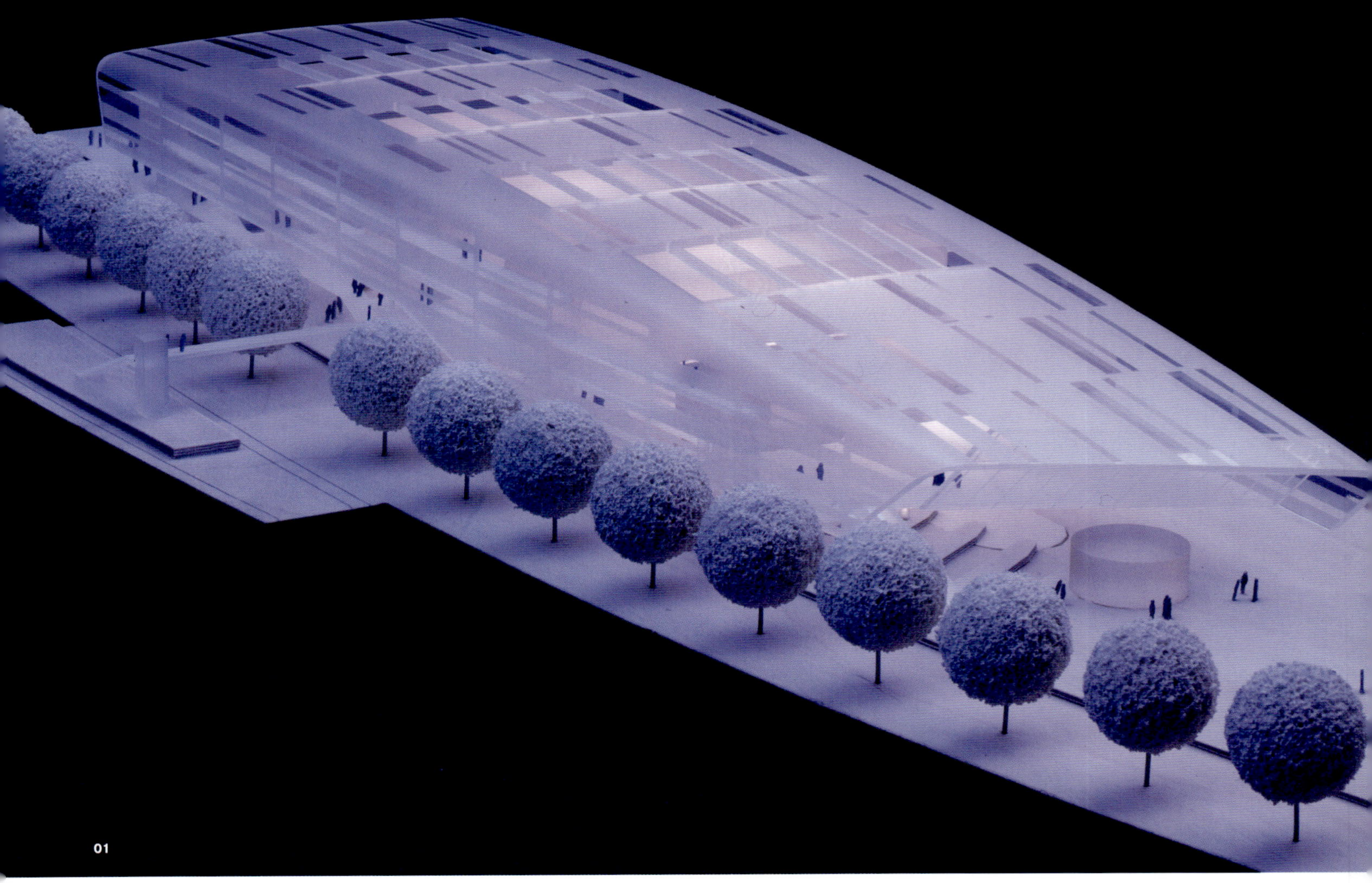

01
02

03

04

01

Central Bus Station, Munich
Competition model
Architect: Auer+Weber+Assoziierte
Scale: 1:500
Photo: Auer+Weber+Assoziierte

02

Herz-Jesu Church, Munich
Presentation Model
Architect: Allmann Sattler Wappner Architekten
Scale: 1:100
Photo: Can Cobanli

03

Süddeutscher Verlag Office Building, Munich
Competition model
Architect: ASW Architekten
Scale: 1:500
Photo: Can Cobanli

04

Laboratory Building, SKW Trostberg
Competition model
Architect: Henn Architekten
Scale: 1:500
Photo: Henn Architekten

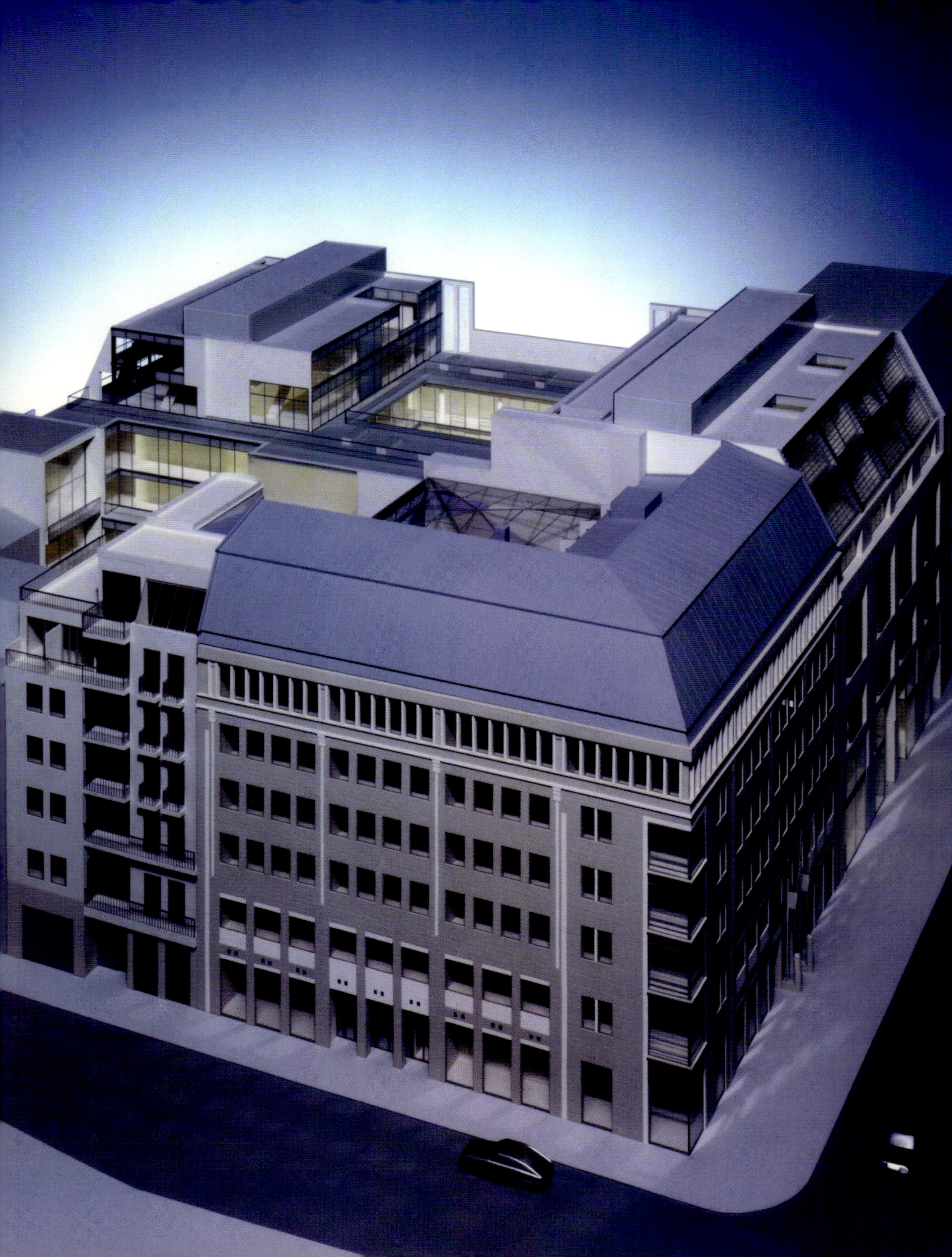

Rüdiger Hammerschmidt
Berlin

New development of Hungarian and Polish embassies
and one other office building, 2000
Architect: Deubzer König Architekten
Scale: 1:100
Material: Hollow construction of perspex and
polystyrene, with partial interior lighting
Photo: Antonia Weiße

www.r-hammerschmidt.de

Rüdiger Hammerschmidt, a qualified architect and graduate of Berlin's Technical University, began his career in premises in the Berlin borough of Charlottenburg, where he opened his first architectural model-making workshop in 1973.

His work ranges from models of Berlin's famous 1920s housing estates, now exhibited all over the world, to competition models produced in the period after the fall of the Berlin Wall. These include context models of the government quarter in the Spreebogen area, the quarters around Potsdamer Platz and Pariser Platz and on Museum Island, and detailed section models of prominent individual buildings that characterise the physiognomy of Berlin's post-1990 urban development. In addition, Hammerschmidt still produces purpose-built representations for competitions, presentations and exhibitions.

During the thirty years since he opened his workshop, his bureau's production methods and raw materials have changed. While his first architectural models were made of balsa wood, quality solid woods, Finnish wood pulp board and plastics are now used as well. The severe style of representation has been retained – though admittedly, the architecture of early modernism automatically draws attention to proportions, making it easier to fulfil the stipulation that an architectural model should leave comparison with reality to the imagination. It may be a consequence of their fine aesthetics that even scale reconstructions of 1920s buildings permit the observer to take an imagined walk along these sweeping façades. Although using different materials and methods of representation, Hammerschmidt extends this restraint even to current competition models. The only difference between his wooden scale models for the Federal Economics Ministry, the expressive power of which he entrusts to the material's cuboid arrangements, and individual models that, from foundation to roof-edge, draw the gaze towards their proportions, is the nuance with which the subject is interpreted.

01 / 02 / 03 ....

WOGA Buildings on Lehniner Platz
for the permanent exhibition at the Art Library of Berlin
Architect: Erich Mendelsohn
Scale: 1:100
Material: Acrylic glass, wood, polystyrene
Photos: Knud Petersen and R. Hammerschmidt

03

01 
02

01

Former Congress Hall in Berlin-Tiergarten
Architect: Hugh Stubbins; after the south ring beam
collapsed, reconstructed by architects
Hans-Peter Störl and Wolf-Rüdiger Borchardt,
both Berlin
Scale: 1:100
Material: Wood, acrylic glass, polystyrene
Photo: Knud Petersen

02/03/04

Zollernhof, Unter den Linden, Berlin
New development of side wings and rear wing on
Mittelstrasse and restoration and reconstruction
of the front building on Unter den Linden
Architect: Thomas Baumann, Berlin
Scale: 1:100, partial model of interior courtyard 1:50
Photos: Antonia Weiße

01

02

01

KPM site, office building for the Federal Health
Associations, Berlin
Architect: Braun & Voigt Planung und
Projektmanagement GmbH
Scale: 1:200
Material: Polystyrene, perspex
Façades including window apertures, frames
and joint structuring CNC-milled
Photo: Antonia Weiße

02

New Master Plan for Museum Island, Berlin
Cutaway model
Architect: David Chipperfield, Hilmer & Sattler,
Heinz Tesar
Scale: 1:100
Material: Natural solid maple wood and maple veneer
Photo: Chipperfield practice

03

Schifffahrtsufer, Spandau, Berlin
Plan for a new housing development
Architect: Jürgen Sawade and Erwin Eickhoff
Scale: 1:200
Material: Wood, acrylic glass, polystyrene
Photo: Knud Petersen

01

Weisse Stadt

Siemenstadt

Lage in der Stadt

02

03

01

1920s Housing Estates Today
White City in Reinickendorf
Exhibition at the Bauhaus Archive, Berlin
Architect: Ahrends and Büning
Scale: 1:50
Material: Wood, acrylic glass, polystyrene
Photo: R. Hammerschmidt

02

1920s Housing Estates Today
Siemensstadt, *Battleship* on Jungfernheideweg
Exhibition at the Bauhaus Archive, Berlin
Architect: Hans Scharoun
Scale: 1:50
Photo: R. Hammerschmidt

03 / 04

Former headquarters of Berliner Sparkasse
on Mühlendamm, Berlin
Historical model from the Construction and Transport
Museum at Hamburger Bahnhof
Scale: 1:50
Material: Wood, metal, glass
Photos: Deutsches Technikmuseum, Berlin

04

01
02

01/02/03/04 ....
Zeughaus, Unter den Linden, Berlin
Dismountable working model
Client: Federal Office for Building and Regional Planning
Scale: 1:50
Material: Plaster, casting resin, silicone rubber
Photos: R. Hammerschmidt

Wolfgang Hannemann
Oldenburg

www.hannemann-modellbau.de

RWTH Aachen University
Architect: RKW Düsseldorf
Scale: 1:1,000
Photo: Holger Knauf, Düsseldorf

For Wolfgang Hannemann, model-making is a craft in the traditional eighteenth-century sense, when each finished piece was a unique item tailored entirely to the customer's requirements. That is precisely how Hannemann's workshop develops commissioned architectural models, by combining specialist qualifications, technical experience, precision craft skills and creative execution. The models are based on the architect's draft plan, but it is the presentation impact desired by the client and the external presentation that determine the model's design.

Hannemann's work is focused mainly on revealing the impact and creative quality or functionality of a design idea. We are meant to be amazed. That is why the architectural model as an enthralling object can sometimes be an end in itself. In the case of everyday consumer items, too, experience shows that people buy the packaging rather than the actual product. Models that fulfil this sensual function often go far beyond a reduction in scale. Consequently, Hannemann does not simply build architectural models to plan, but engages closely with the building and the client.

In this context, the ability to put oneself in the observer's place is fundamental. Only from this perspective is it possible to develop the overall concept for a model jointly with the customer and to express the thinking behind the design in the miniature representation. The classical mode of representation is the white model that captivates through its proportions alone. Another possibility is to use fine nuances of colour that may be produced by lighting effects and that may occasionally culminate in glaring tones. Hannemann's models reveal a fine sense of proportion and effect, so that each colour and the way it is coordinated is just as unique as the composition of the model itself. In this workshop, colouring and material are seen as tools of trade that take the craftsman closer to the architecture of the original.

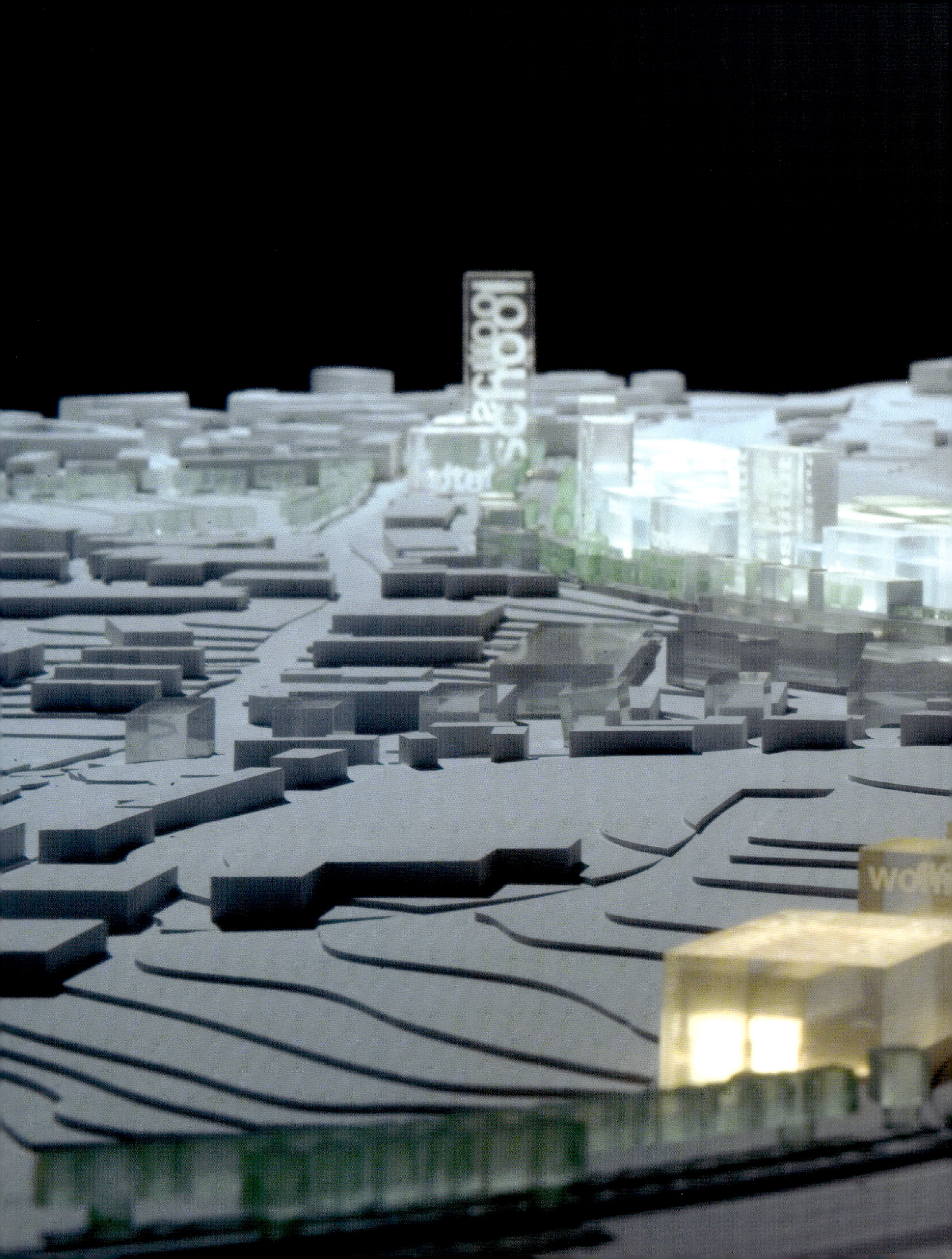
School
after
water

forschung
campus
wohnen
wohnen
wohnen
wohnen
cafe
campus

01

02

Page 98/99
RWTH Aachen University
Architect: RKW Düsseldorf
Scale: 1:1,000
Photo: Holger Knauf, Düsseldorf

01/02/03/04
Baltic Arena, Gdansk
Architect: RKW Architekten, Düsseldorf
Scale: 1:250
Photos: Holger Knauf, Düsseldorf

Oman Resort
Architect: Reardon Smith Architects/Chapman Taylor,
London
Scale: 1:2,000
Photo: Holger Knauf, Düsseldorf

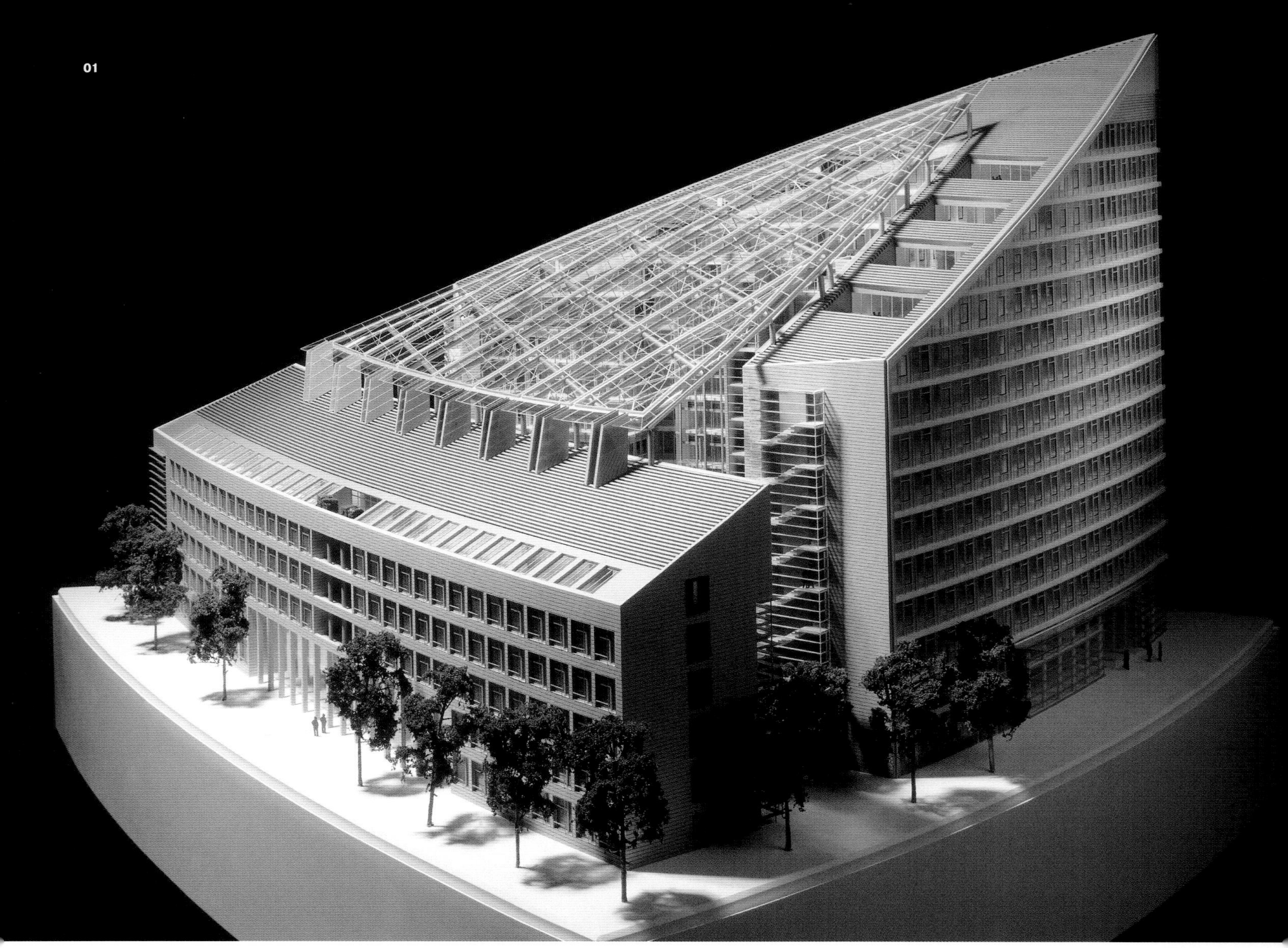

03

04

01 / 02

MainTriangel
Architect: Novotny + Mähner, Offenbach
Scale: 1:100
Photos: Christian Richters, Münster

03 / 04

Concept Study
Architect: Kresing, Münster
Scale: 1:500
Photos: Christian Richters, Münster

Office Building
Architect: Daniel Libeskind
Scale: 1:200
Photo: Thomas Riehle, Cologne

01

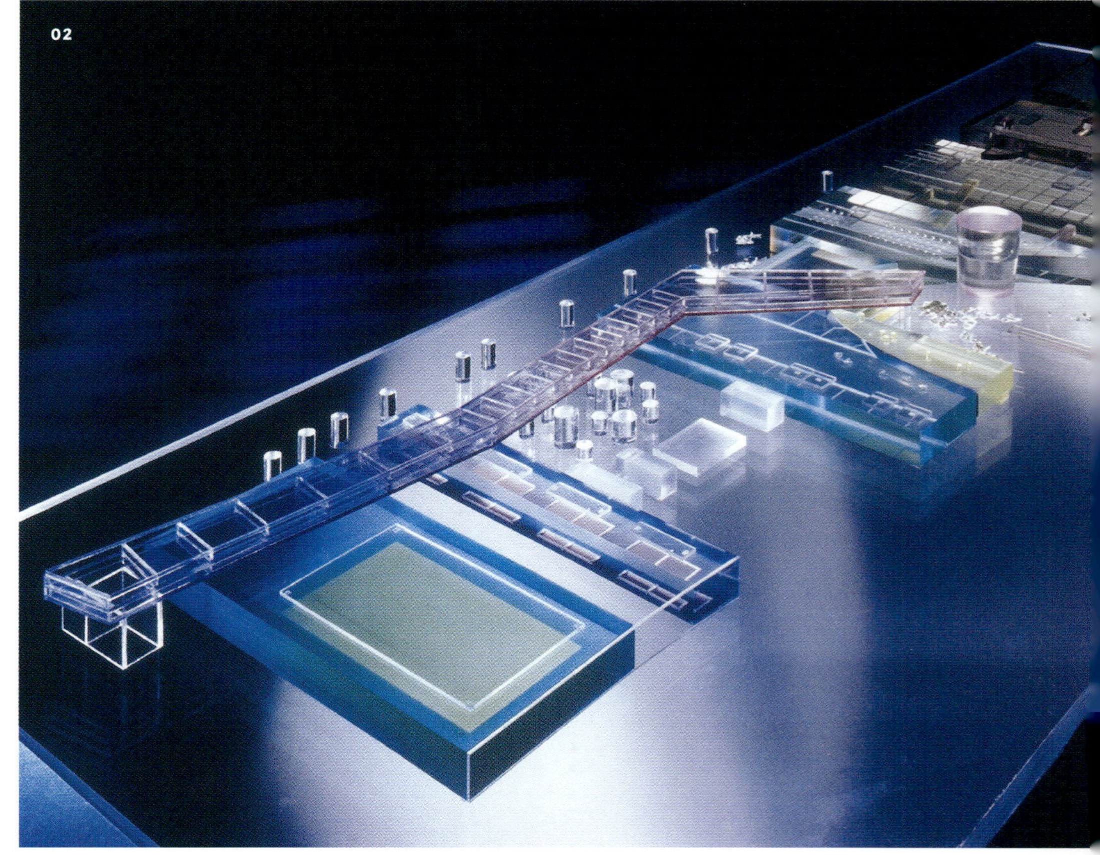
02

Page 102/103
ECE Shopping Centre, Braunschweig
Architect: Grazioli + Muthesius Berlin
Scale: 1:160
Photo: Axel Schmidt, Ratingen

01
Spreeufer Centre Berlin
Architect: RKW Düsseldorf
Scale: 1:1,000
Photo: Holger Knauf, Düsseldorf

02/03
Dunapark Budapest
Architect: Kresing, Münster
Scale: 1:2,000
Photos: Christian Richters, Münster

04
Office Building
Architect: mfi AG Essen
Scale: 1:1,000
Photo: Thomas Riehle, Cologne

01

02

01

NRW Bank, Düsseldorf
Architect: RKW Düsseldorf
Scale: 1:200
Photo: Holger Knauf, Düsseldorf

02

Nova Eventis, Leipzig/Halle
Architect: ECE Hamburg
Scale: 1:50
Photo: Hannemann Modellbau

03

Hitachi, Duisburg
Architect: Bahl + Partner, Hagen
Scale: 1:200
Photo: Axel Schmidt, Ratingen

01 / 02 / 03

Egyptian Museum, Cairo
Architect: KSP Engel und Zimmermann
Scale: 1:1,000
Photos: Axel Schmidt, Ratingen

04

Dubai Pearl
Architect: Chapman Taylor, London
Scale: 1:200
Photo: Axel Schmidt, Ratingen

01

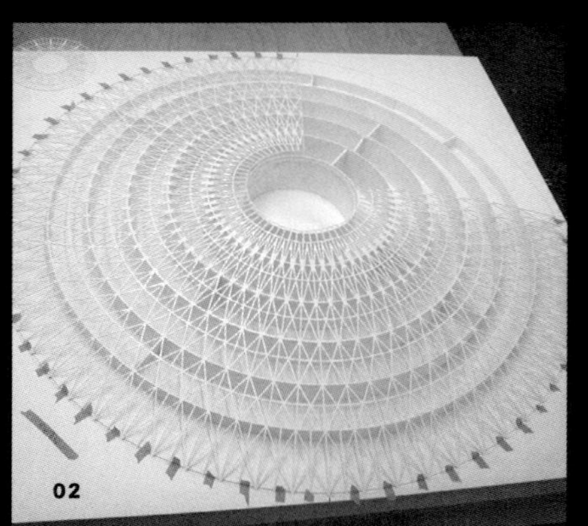

02

03

04

05

06

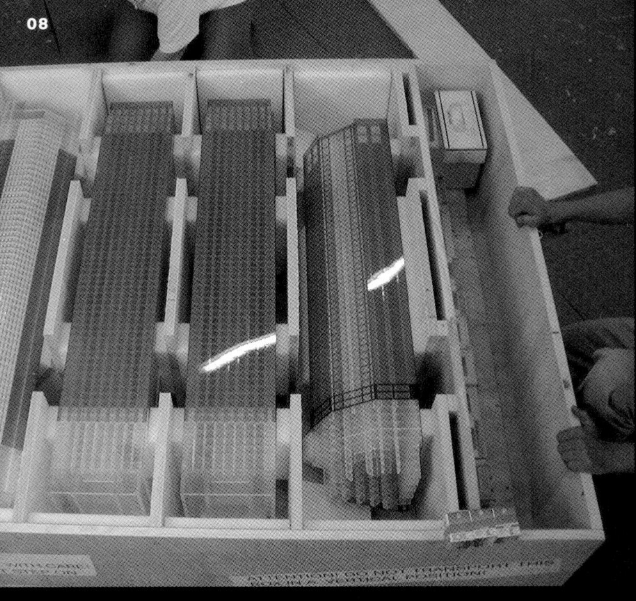

Dubai Pearl
Scale: 1:200 (3.50 by 3.50 metres)
Prototype model

01 ....
Assembling the base plate

02 ....
Assembling the cupola segments

03 ....
Assembling the interior segment

04 ....
Light installation

05 ....
Adjusting the individual elements

06 ....
Installing traffic lanes

07 ....
Inserting the towers

08 ....
Packing for transport by air

Hauke Helmer and Ulrich Mangold
Berlin

werk 5 Mangold Helmer GmbH

www.werk5.com

World Trade Center, New York City, 2002
First prize in competition
Architect: Studio Libeskind
Scale: 1:1,200
Material: Acrylic, Necuron
Technique: Three- and five-axial CNC, engraved,
acrylic matted and polished, Minilux
Photo: werk 5

Since its foundation in 1995 werk5, which operates mainly in the field of architectural and design model-making, has seen itself as a combined laboratory and workshop, a »learning and teaching business«. Accordingly, its engineers, most of whom are skilled artisans, continuously develop the aesthetics of models and employ new technologies. Phases during which materials and representational options are tested often give rise to unusual manufacturing processes. »Modelling in the material« is a process that emerged from many experiments. Sometimes meticulously detailed variant models of various segments are made before the scale architectural model is constructed. The segments may show different ways of working a façade profile with the aim of judging their visual impact. This approach is in line with werk5's mission to give shape to the core idea of the plan in the model and render it visually comprehensible. The aim is to enable the »poetry of the digital« to be sensed and heard in the model, despite its technical perfection. Such experiments are above all expedient. They make the expressive power inherent in the design clear to the model-maker and to the client, who is always involved in the work processes. This haptic advice enables the customer to play a powerful role in codetermining the model's aesthetics.

Each model thus acquires its own unmistakable character. Although werk5 has recourse to a wealth of different materials to achieve this, it develops new combinations of materials and processing variations as required for the task in hand. Customers, be they architects, property developers, designers, artists or event managers, get to see the results of the different stages of co-development, from individual pieces and special parts via prototypes and working models through to the presentation model.

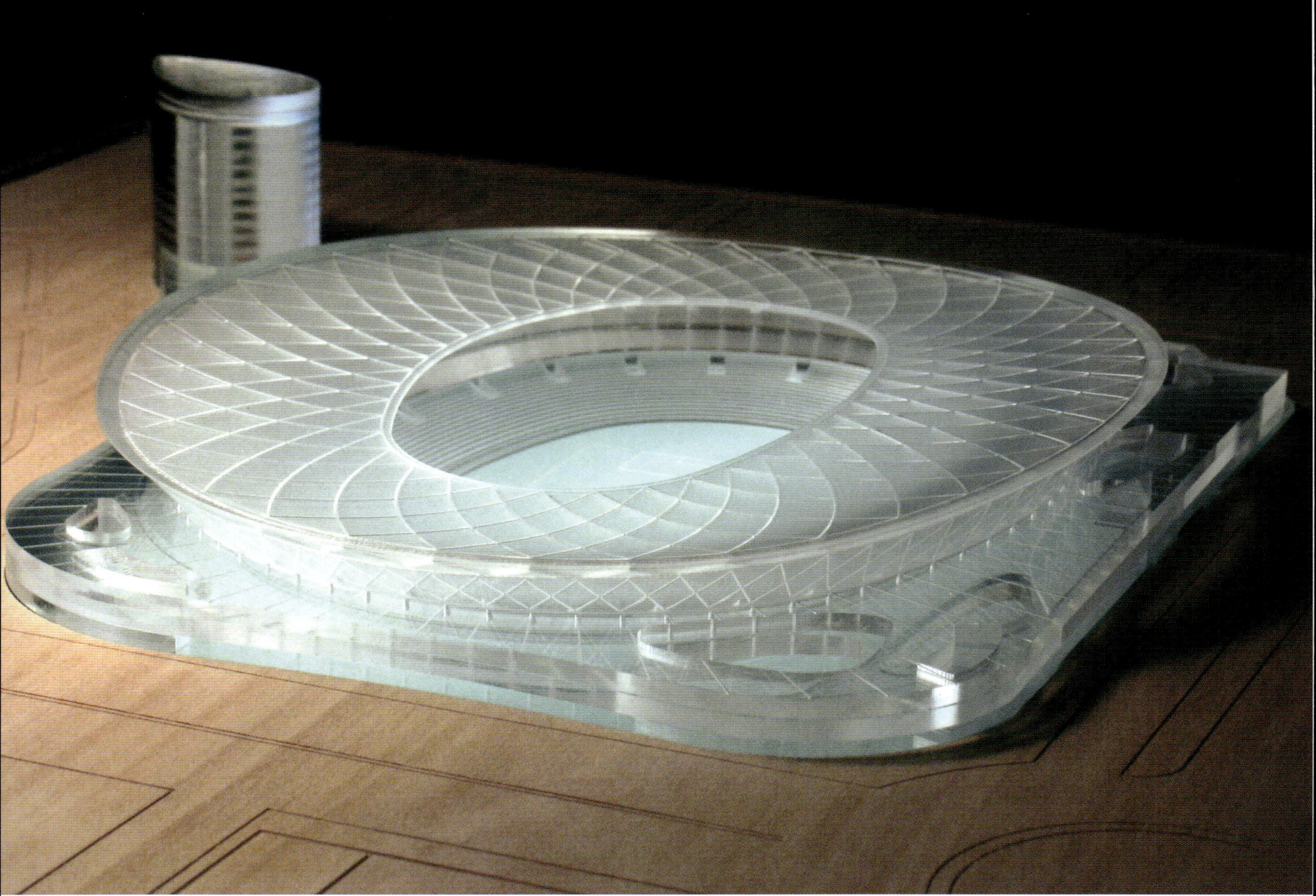

02

03

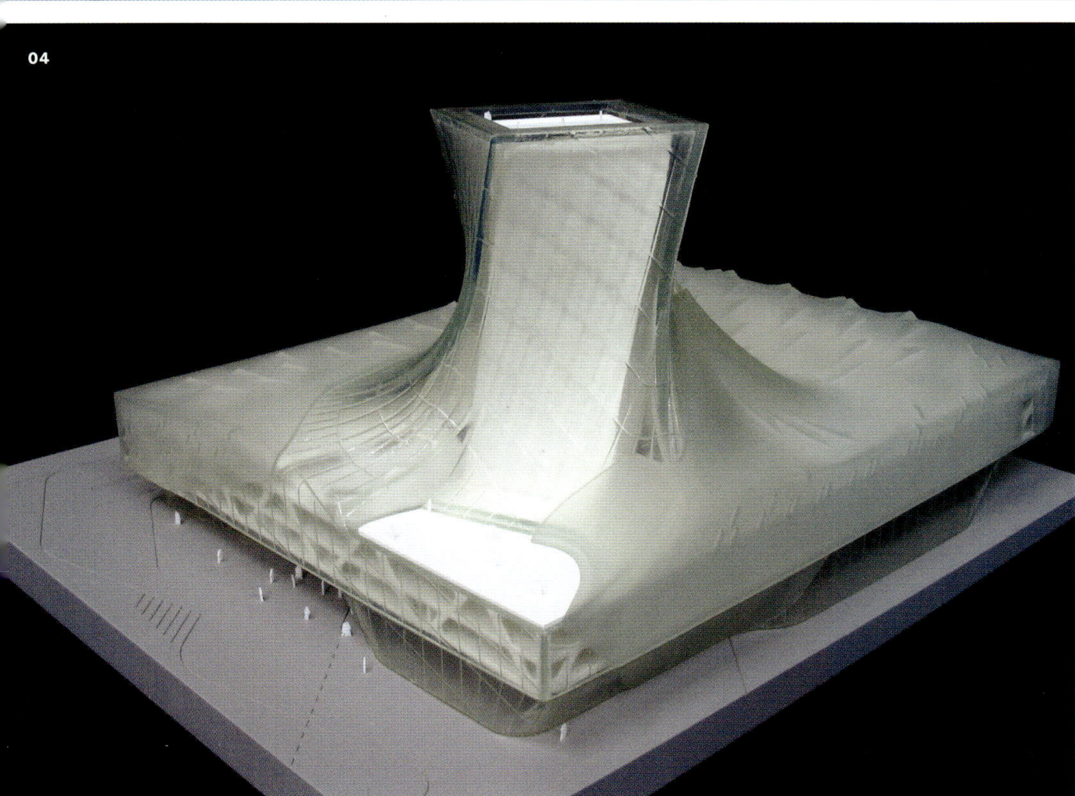

04

01

Stadium, Valencia
Competition model
First prize in competition
Architect: von Gerkan, Marg und Partner
Scale: 1:1,000
Material: Acrylic
Technique: Three-axial CNC
Photo: werk 5

02

Stadium, Munich
Competition model 2001
Architect: KSP Engel und Zimmermann
Scale: 1:200
Material: Plastics, acrylic, mirror
Technique: Three-axial CNC, spotlights
Photo: Gerhard Kassner

03

Upper Eastside, Berlin, 2006
Marketing suite display, Berlin
Architect: von Gerkan, Marg und Partner,
Kahlfeldt Architekten, Augusto Romano Burelli
Scale: 1:75
Material: Rigid polyurethane foam, acrylic,
nickel silver, Necuron
Technique: Structured as travertine,
digitally controlled LED lighting
Photo: werk 5

04

National Library, Prague
Commended
Architect: Holzer Kobler
Scale: 1:500
Material: UV hardening Duroplast
Technique: 3-D plot, partially glass bead-blasted,
deep drawn
Photo: werk 5

01

Cologne Oval Offices on
Gustav-Heinemann-Ufer, Cologne
Presentation model 2005
Client: MEAG
Architect: Sauerbruch Hutton Architekten
Scale: 1:500
Material: Screen-printed stainless steel,
plastic, lighting
Photo: werk 5

02

Office Building, Hamburg
Presentation model 2005
Client: Momeni Immobilien
Architect: BRT Architekten Bothe Richter Teherani
Scale: 1:100
Material: Acrylic, diverse plastics, soapstone
Lighting: Lightsticks
Photo: werk 5

01

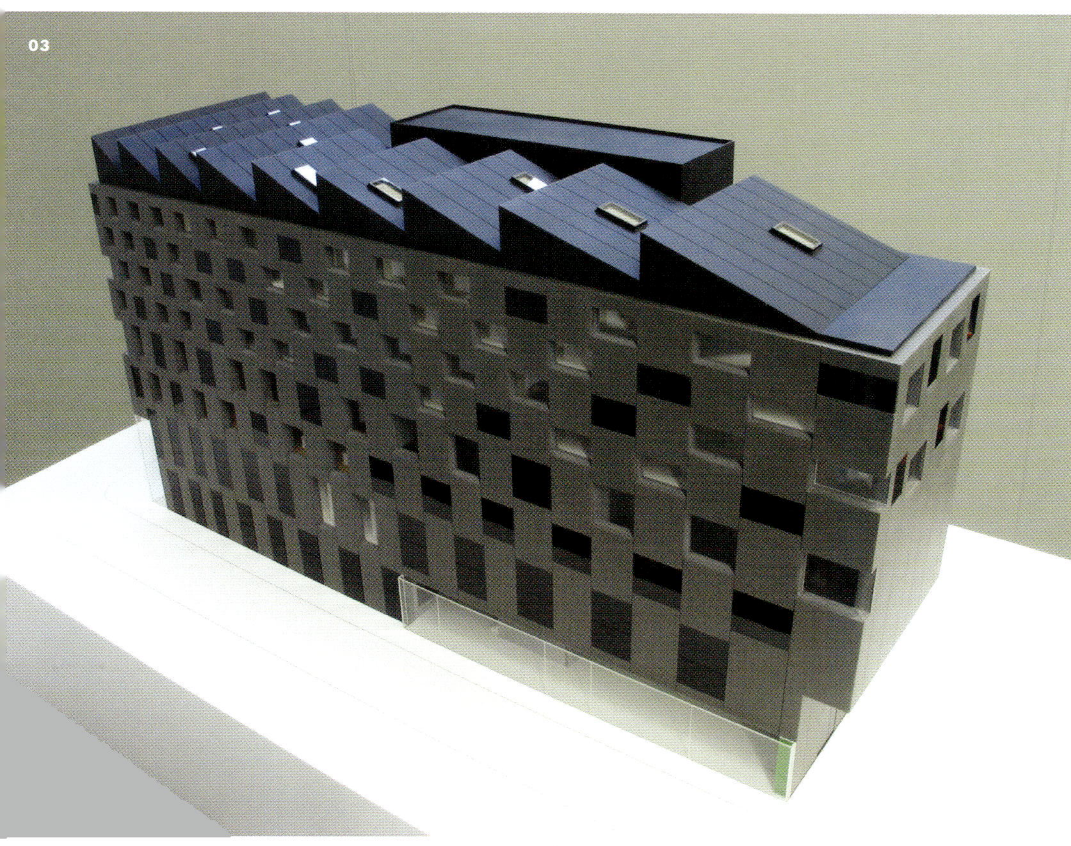

01

Jewish Community Centre, Berlin, 2003
Architect: Studio Libeskind
Scale: 1:200
Material: Coloured acrylic, nickel silver, beechwood ply
Technique: Three- and five-axial CNC, engraved,
microetching, lightsticks
Photo: werk 5

02

TOC Düsseldorf
Architect: Rhode Kellermann Wawrowsky
Scale: 1:100
Material: Acrylic, mirror foil, rigid polyurethane foam
Technique: Five-axial CNC
Photo: werk 5

03

SOP, London
Architect: Adjaye Associates Ltd.
Scale: 1:50
Material: Necuron, coloured acrylic
Technique: CNC
Photo: werk 5

U/S BARMBEK

04

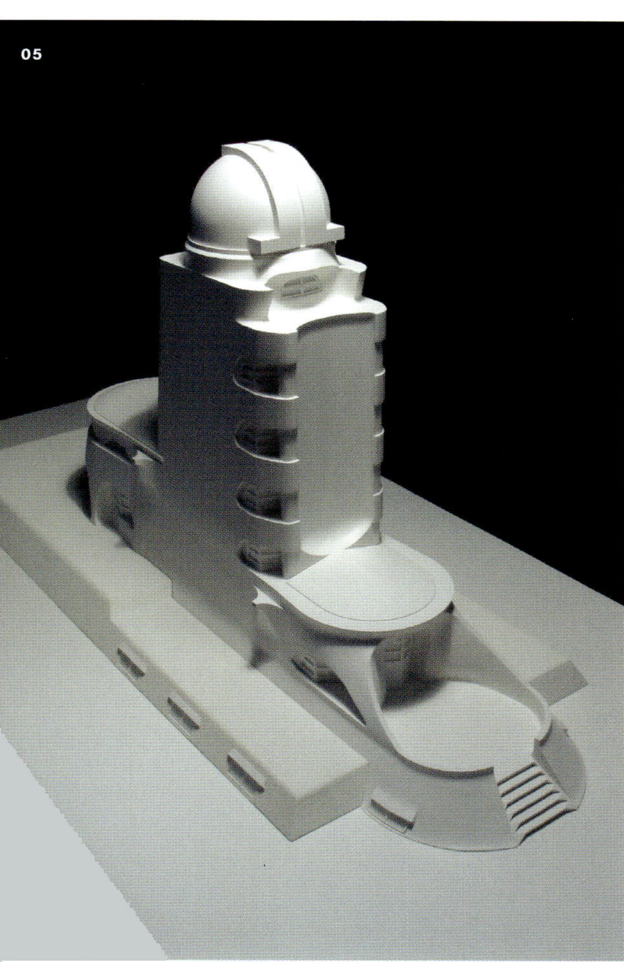

05

01

Barmbek Station
Presentation model 2005
Architect: APPlan Vielmo Architekten
Scale: 1:50
Material: Deep-drawn acrylic, aluminium, wood, LED
Technique: Three-axial CNC, deep drawn
Photo: werk 5

02

Sparkasse Oberhausen, interior spiral staircase
Competition model 2003
Architect: Sauerbruch Hutton Architekten
Scale: 1:500
Material: Solid pear wood, acrylic, nickel silver,
rigid polyurethane foam
Technique: Microetching
Photo: werk 5

03

Interior of Pheidias's workshop
Presentation model 2002
Die Griechische Klassik (Greek Classicism)
exhibition, Martin-Gropius-Bau,
Berlin and Archaeological Museum, Athens
Client: Antikensammlung Berlin
Scale: 1:50
Material: Rigid polyurethane foam, solid pear wood,
acrylic
Technique: Three- and five-axial CNC, engraved
Photo: werk 5

04

Church Altar, Florence
Competition model 1997
Architect: Prof. Klaus Theo Brenner Architekten
Scale: 1:500
Material: Solid pear wood
Technique: CNC
Photo: werk 5

05

Einstein Tower, Potsdam, Display model
Client: Display model for the Historical Museum, Bern,
2005-06
Architect: Erich Mendelsohn, 1920
Scale: 1:50
Material: Rigid polyurethane foam, paint
Technique: Five-axial CNC
Photo: werk 5

01

02

03

04

01 / 02

Cité du Design in St. Etienne
Working model 2004 and final
Architect: Fin Geipel LIN
Scale: 1:333
Material: Nickel silver, brass
Technique: Microetched
Photos: werk 5

03

Villa Luise, Mannheim, 2003
Architect: Fischer Architekten
Scale: 1:50
Material: Solid wood, pear
Technique: 2-D and five-axial CNC, engraved
Photo: werk 5

04

Tresor Tower, Berlin
Working model 1996
Architect: Röhrs und Beyer Architekten with werk 5
Scale: 1:200
Material: Brass, nickel silver, acrylic, lighting
Technique: Microetching
Photo: werk 5

01

02

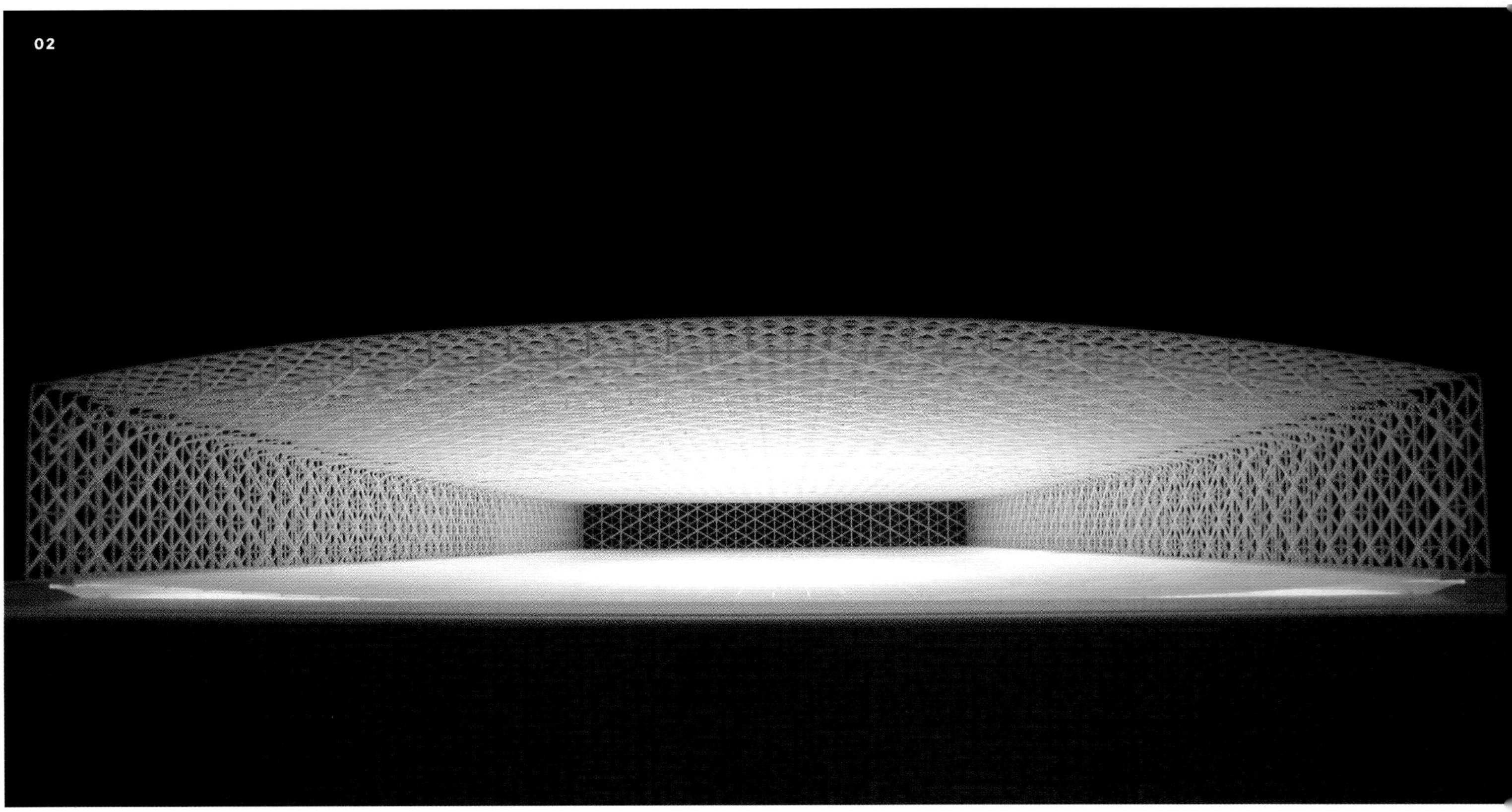

03

04

01

Office Building, Hamburg
Presentation model 2005
First prize in competition
Architect: Cogiton und J. Mayer H.
Scale: 1:100
Material: Polystyrene, acrylic
Technique: Five-axial CNC
Photo: werk 5

02

Cité du Design in St. Etienne
Architect: Fin Geipel LIN
Scale: 1:100
Material: Polystyrene
Technique: CNC, lightsticks
Photo: werk 5

03

Metropol Parasol, Seville
Architect: J. Mayer H.
Scale: 1:200
Material: Acrylic
Technique: Fibre optic lighting, lightstick system
Photo: werk 5

04

Competition, Oberanger, Munich
Architect: Fin Geipel LIN
Scale: 1:500
Material: Coloured acrylic
Technique: Microetched, light
Photo: werk 5

01

02

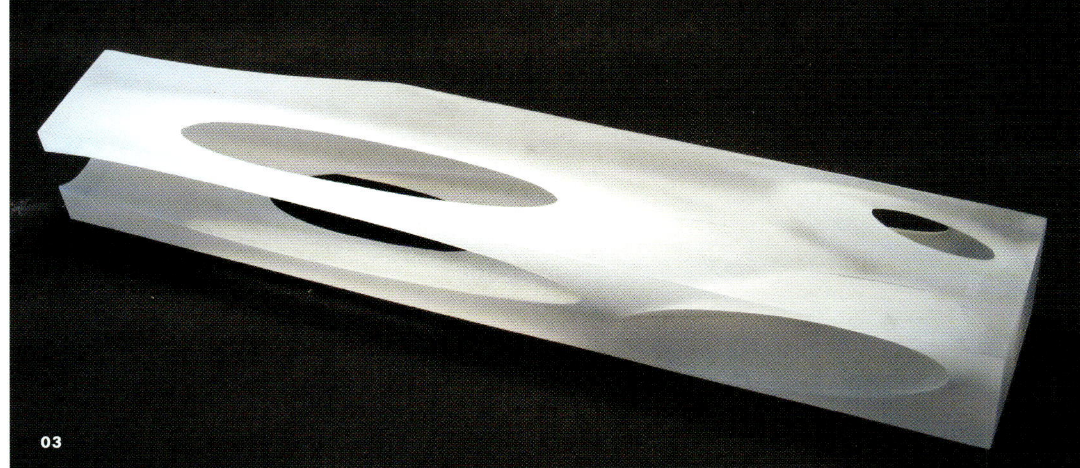

03

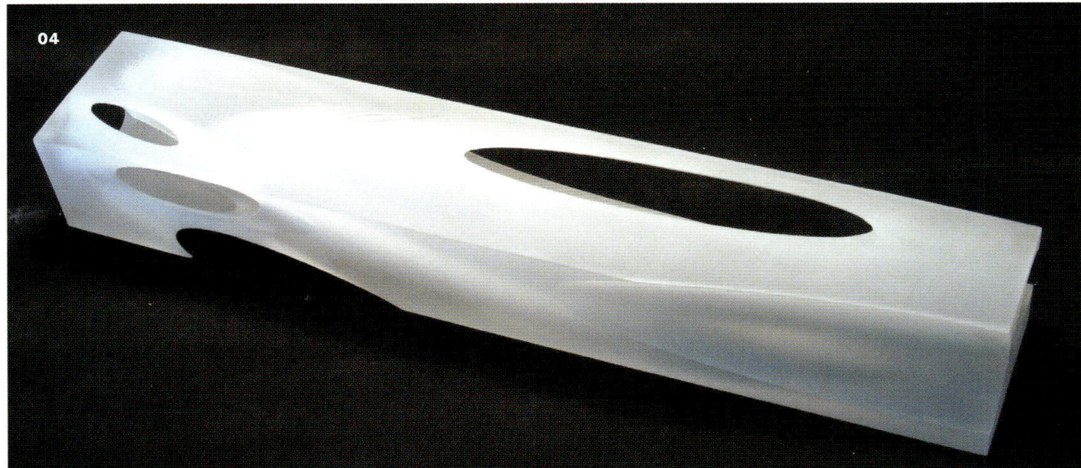

04

01/02

Performing Arts Center, Beijing
Architect: von Gerkan, Marg und Partner
Scale: 1:300
Material: Aluminium, precision acrylic glass
Technique: Five-axial CNC, lightsticks
Photos: werk 5

03/04

Multiple, 2005
Exhibition architecture for *25*
Client: Deutsche Guggenheim
Architect: Zaha Hadid
Scale: 1:40
Material: Polyurethane
Technique: CNC, cast model
Photos: werk 5

05

Church, Wünsdorf
Architect: GRAFT International
Scale: 1:250
Material: Acrylic
Technique: Five-axial CNC,
surface glass bead-blasted
Photo: werk 5

05

01

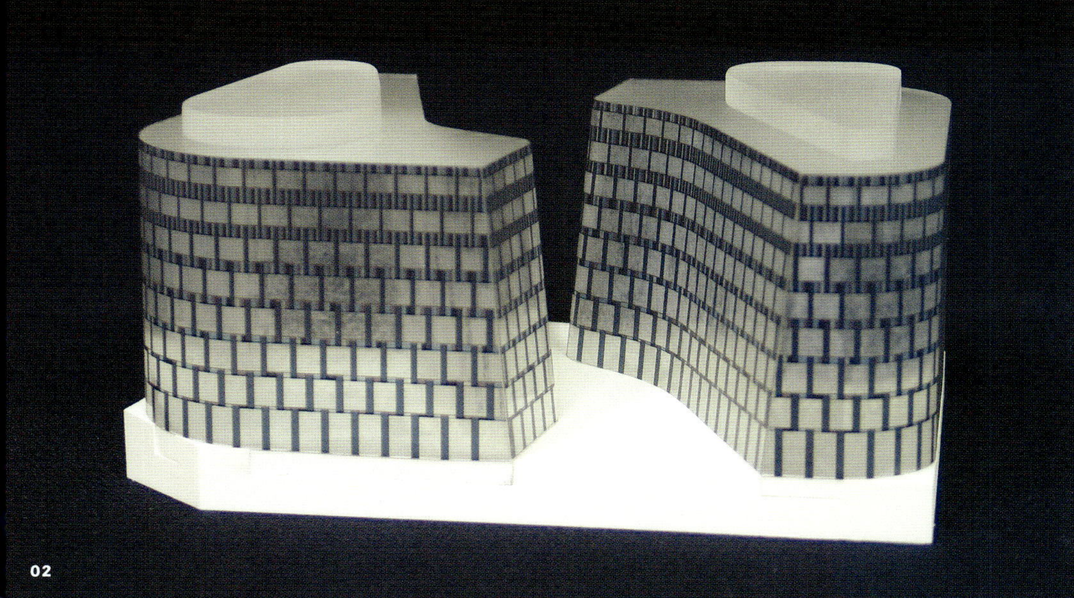

01

KFW Bank, Frankfurt am Main
Presentation model
First prize in competition
Architekt: Sauerbruch Hutton Architekten
Scale: 1:100
Material: Coloured acrylic
Technique: Laser cut
Photo: werk 5

02

Lehrter Urban Quarter, Berlin
Second prize in competition
Architect: Sauerbruch Hutton Architekten
Scale: 1:500
Material: Acrylic
Technique: Five-axial CNC
Photo: werk 5

03

Münster
Competition model
Architect: Sauerbruch Hutton Architekten
Scale: 1:500
Material: Coloured acrylic, wood
Technique: CNC
Photo: werk 5

04

Überseezentrum, Hamburg
Architect: Sauerbruch Hutton Architekten
Scale: 1:500
Material: Coloured acrylic
Technique: Five-axial CNC
Photo: werk 5

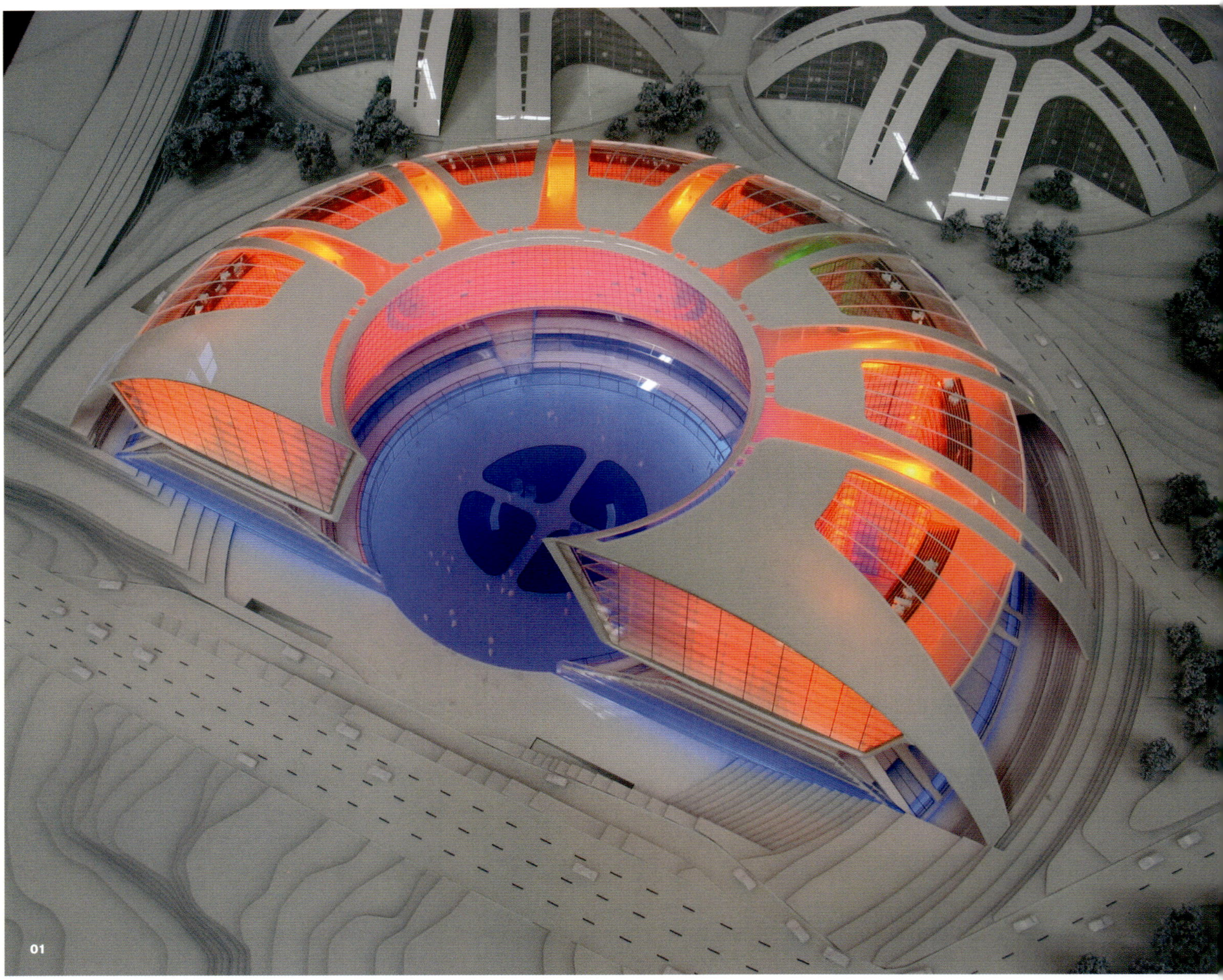

01

02

03

04

01/02/03/04/05 ....

Interactive Model in the »Interactive Cube«
Setun Hills, lighting situations
Client: INTECO
Architect: BRT Hamburg
Execution: werk 5, Macina, Banse
Scale: 1:600
Material: Acrylic, nickel silver
Technique: Deep-drawn, five-axial CNC, LED lighting
Photos: werk 5, Jörg Hempel

The model's lighting changes in correlation to
the information on the transparent screen.

While the animated graphics are running, the control
system makes the relevant areas of the model light up.

The viewer can retrieve information and activate the
lighting in the individual parts of the model selectively.

05

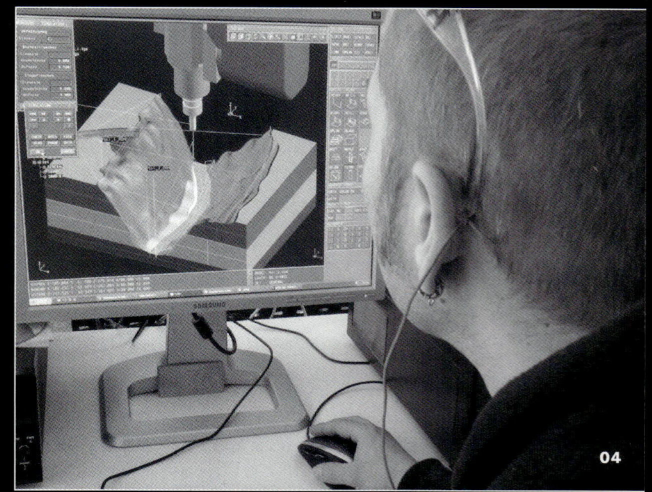

05

06

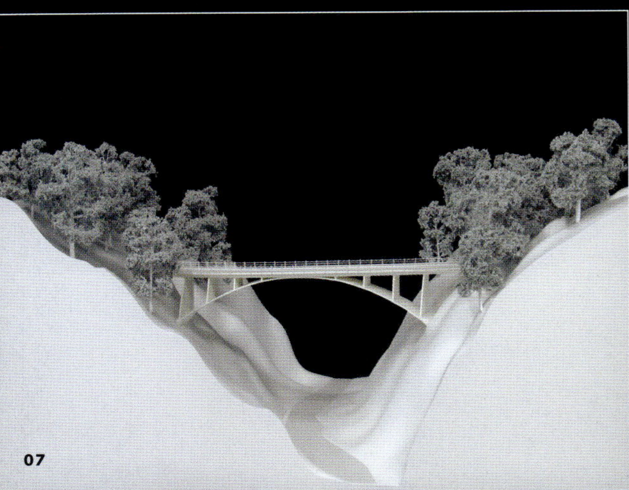

07

From idea to model

01 ....
Design, sketch:
Material samples and working models or test pieces
serve as an aid to decision-making during the
conception phase.

02 ....
3-D CAD, rendering:
Depending on requirements, a digital 2-D or 3-D model
forms the basis for actual implementation of the design.

03 ....
Material:
Skilful selection enables the potential of the material
to be fully utilised so as to give the model the desired
effect.

04 ....
CAM:
Computer Aided Manufacturing: the milling operation is
programmed and first simulated virtually.

05 ....
CNC:
CNC stands for Computerised Numerical Control.
The CNC machine calculates the most efficient work
process.

06 ....
Finishing:
Finally, careful manual work is crucial to the model's
quality and aesthetic impact.

07 ....
Model:
The finished object is the result of a joint development
process of werk 5 and the client.

Siegi Jarnig
Munich

www.modellbau-jarnig.de

Measured by the generally rapid pace of technical development, this company, founded in 1973, is already something of a long-established enterprise. Jarnig who worked in an architect's bureau for a lengthy period and set up in business on his own after taking his master's examination in architectural model-making. In the beginning, he made his models by hand. This dexterity shaped his profile and established his reputation. The aptitude as a craftsman that he showed at that time has enabled him to retain the loyalty of major customers such as *Flughafengesellschaft München*. Over the years, naturalistic rendition of reality has evolved as the characteristic interpretative feature of his works. The customer's requirement determines whether a model is more functional or more detailed. Jarnig sees his many years' experience as an ideal prerequisite for advising customers on execution, because as a model-maker, he knows how a representation can impact on the observer. In this regard he finds it important to embody a building so that it has visual appeal and that everyone understands it at first sight.

The style of design that has evolved on this basis is essentially naturalistic. However, its particular articulation is adjusted to the purpose for which the individual model is intended. Jarnig's aim is always to make it as easy as possible to visualise the idea for a building while simultaneously maintaining a distance from the model, as if it were a toy, a model railway perhaps. On looking at the architect's plan he sees the model in his mind's eye – and on the computer he builds a CAD plan just like an architect would. Is he making a model or building a real house? Jarnig's models are preliminary works of architecture.

Jarnig produces a variety of models ranging from competition models such as those for BMW to sales models for real estate companies, from individual buildings to context models for town planning purposes. This wide range shows how relative the plasticity of a scale representation can be. Material is a determining factor here. Jarnig works in various materials, but prefers working with plastic.

BMW Group
Mini Brand Architecture
Presentation model
Scale: 1:43
Material: Plastic, perspex
Photo: Ullrich Ottes, Sebastian Höpfner

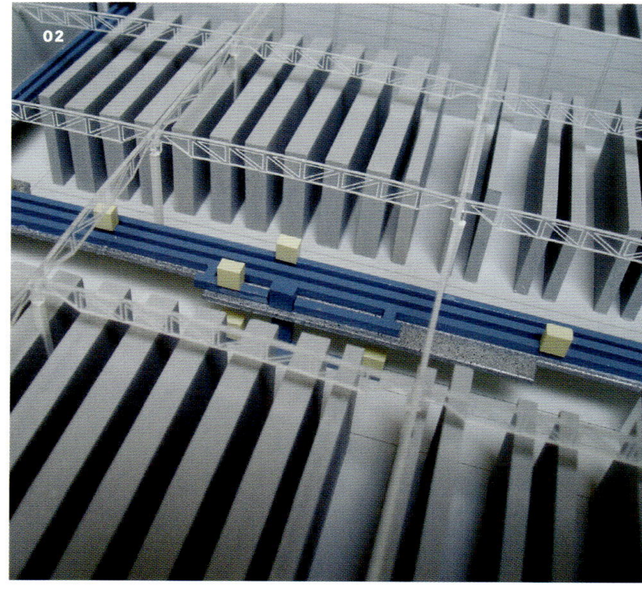

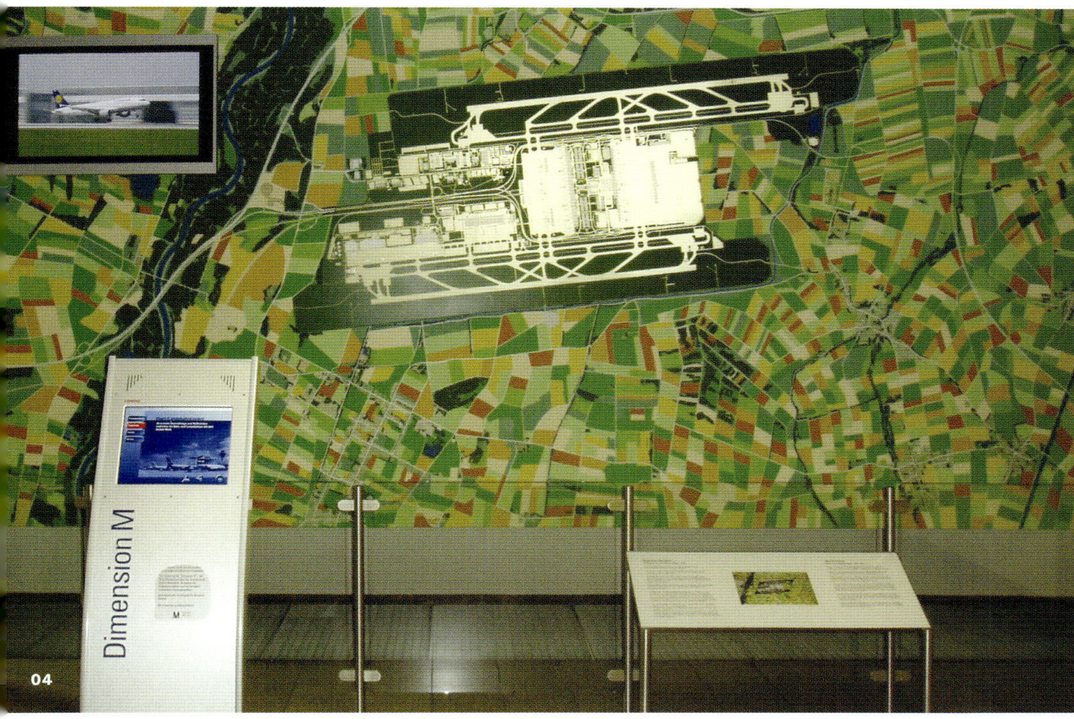

01

BMW Group
Mini Brand Architecture
Illuminated presentation model
Scale: 1:43
Material: Plastic, perspex
Photo: Ullrich Ottes, Sebastian Höpfner

02 / 03

Competition model of ADAC site Munich
Scale: 1:500
Material: Plastic, limewood
Photos: Modellbau Jarnig

04

Munich Airport
Naturalistic overview model
Scale: 1:2,500
Photo: Modellbau Jarnig

05

Munich Airport, Terminals 1 and 2
Scale: 1:500
Photo: Modellbau Jarnig

01

02

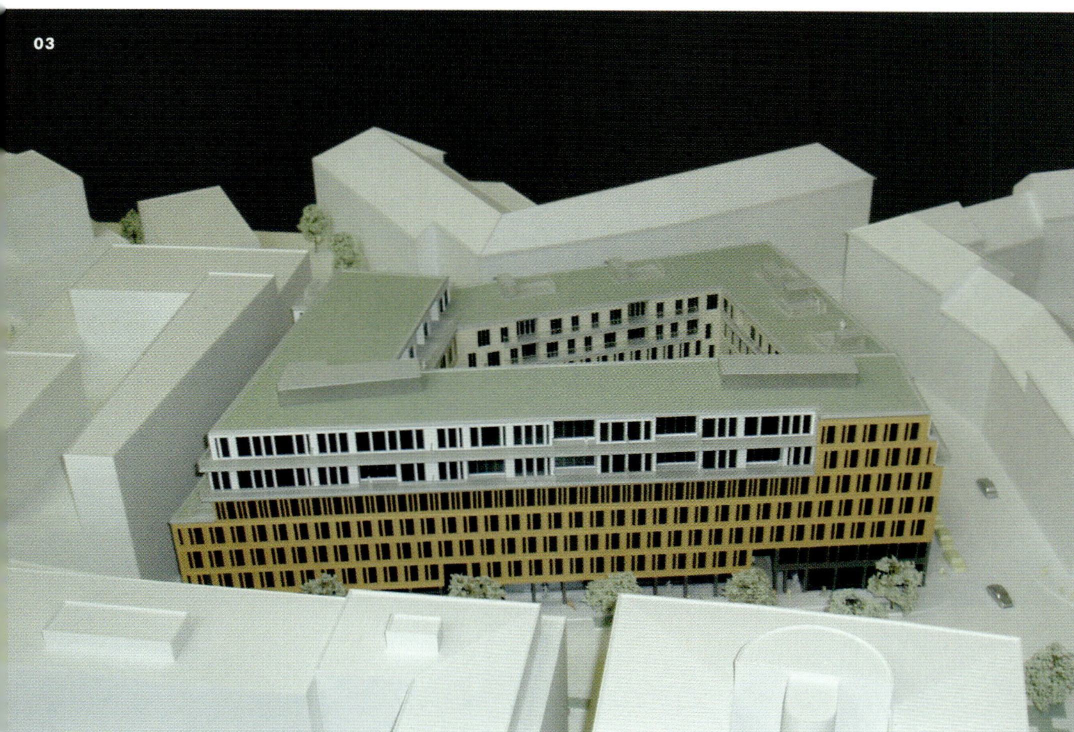

01 / 02

DIBAG, residential care home and
home for the elderly, Ingolstadt
Scale: 1:100
Photos: Michael Volkmann

03 / 04

Wöhr und Bauer GmbH commercial and
residential building, Oberanger, Munich
Scale: 1:200
Photos: Modellbau Jarnig

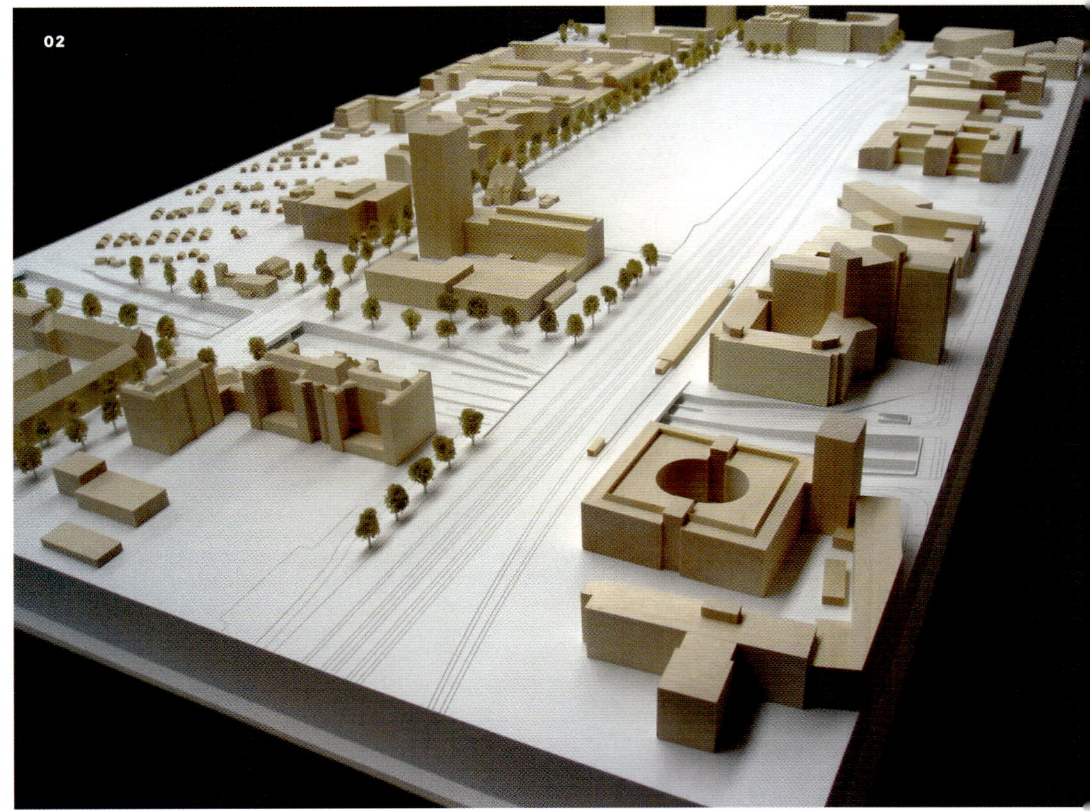

01 / 02

Frankonia Eurobau AG & Co. KG
Lenbach Gardens, Munich
Scale: 1:100
Photos: Modellbau Jarnig

03 / 04

DIBAG, Italian Village
Scale: 1:100
Photos: Modellbau Jarnig

03

04

Michael Kropf

Graz

www.modellbau-kropf.at

Modellbau Kropf was established in 1964. The main focus of the firm's architectural model-making is on producing scale buildings for exhibitions and museums. Some of these haptic architectural bodies are integrated into permanent exhibitions, for instance at the *Kulturhistorisches Museum* and the *Technisches Museum* in Vienna. In addition to model reconstructions and replicas of historical buildings, the company also makes three-dimensional show and presentation models for building projects. These are displayed at international real estate fairs in Cannes or Munich. The captivating quality of these works is realistic representation that is faithful in every detail, from architectural elements to volumes and materials. Even the model of the *Kaiser Franz Joseph Stadtmuseum* in Vienna, designed by Otto Wagner but never built, looks as if it were real. All building components are made separately prior to assembly according to their surface colouring or material (e.g. stone surfaces, metal surfaces) on the basis of building plan data.

This meticulous approach is followed for current competition models, too. In these, however, figural detail is less important. The accent is on overall visual impact and on highlighting striking contrasts. In the *Palazzo Tergesteo a Mare* in Trieste, for example, the entrance is shaped as a bright red buoy to contrast with the milky-white complex. The high level of precision is evident in the design of the horizontal bands on the façade and in the vivid interplay between the elements of the outer skin and the functional, load-bearing elements inside. Nothing is superfluous. This fine rendition of architectural characteristics can also be seen in the model of the rehearsal stage for the Munich *Kammerspiele*. To look at, it could be mistaken for a computer-generated creation, but no virtual reality can be as true to life as historical replicas in all their materiality.

Model of Kaiser Franz Joseph Stadtmuseum, Vienna
Architect: Otto Wagner (1903)
Scale: 1:50
Material: Acrylic glass, polyester casting resin, brass
Client: Historisches Museum der Stadt Wien
Constructed: 1988
Photo: Herbert Schwingenschlögl

03

04

01 / 02

Kaiser Franz Joseph Stadtmuseum, Vienna
Architect: Otto Wagner (1903)
Scale: 1:50
Material: Acrylic glass, polyester casting resin, brass
Client: Historisches Museum der Stadt Wien
Construction: 1988
Photos: Herbert Schwingenschlögl

03 / 04

Octagon, Ephesus, Turkey
Roman, 2nd half of first century AD
Scale: 1:25
Material: Acrylic glass, polyester casting resin
Client: Ephesus Museum, Vienna
Construction: 1978
Photos: Herbert Schwingenschlögl

GOLDMAN & SALATS
GOLDMAN & SALATSCH

Building on Michaelerplatz, Vienna
Client: *Traum und Wirklichkeit* (Dream and Reality)
exhibition
Architect: Adolf Loos (1909-11)
Scale: 1:50
Material: Acrylic glass, polyester casting resin, wood
Construction: 1985
Photo: Herbert Schwingenschlögl

01

02

01

Munich Kammerspiele – Rehearsal Stage
Architect: Prof. Gustav Peichl + Partner, Vienna
Scale: 1:50
Material: Acrylic glass
Photo: Herbert Schwingenschlögl

02

Palazzo Tergesteo a Mare, Trieste
Architect: Prof. Gustav Peichl + Partner,
Prof. Fonatti, Arch. Veselinovic
Scale: 1:100
Material: Acrylic glass, brass
Photo: Herbert Schwingenschlögl

03 / 04

park.gate office building, Munich
Architect: Perret, Reichert, Pranschke, Maluche
Scale: 1:133
Material: Acrylic glass, brass
Photos: Herbert Schwingenschlögl

03

04

Burkhard Lüdtke

Berlin

www.1art-design.de

Student projects
Photo: Gunter Lepkowski

Ever since model-making was introduced as a discipline for students of architecture at Berlin's Technical University twenty years ago, the qualified showcase designer, design graduate and art teacher Burkhard Lüdtke has headed the department. Lüdtke came to academic life after working as a craftsman, and his design company 1ART translates allegedly commonplace items into surprising yet practical three-dimensional shapes. The department is like Lüdtke himself – methodical in approach, unorthodox in implementation. It is the only and last place in a university operation weighed down by theory where architecture students can learn that a design idea, a draft, can only be understood when it is embodied, and that there is no model without a creative aspiration. And it is also the place where they learn to give shape to this creative aspiration.

Lüdtke's seminars are in the nature of workshops. Each semester, a new task is set up which challenges students to go beyond traditional materials and techniques and to experiment with materials that are not typical in model-making. Unusual, three-dimensional interpretative versions of an idea for a building emerge in materials such as corrugated cardboard, sweets or metalworking utensils. Enthusiastic experimentation leads to a creative sense of the multiple ways in which material, colour and structure can be used to showcase volume, surface area and line as the three basic elements of spatial design. The results transcend even what is presented today in the field of perfected model-making. This interplay of craft and playful use of means of expression has gained the students a number of practical commissions. These have included, instead of the customary model in a glass case, a wall-filling relief model of the *Märkisches Viertel* district for the Berlin housing company GESOBAU, various stage decorations and, currently, a model of the *Reichstag* building for the blind. These technically and creatively extraordinary works have been shown in multiple exhibitions, thereby helping the department to international breakthrough.

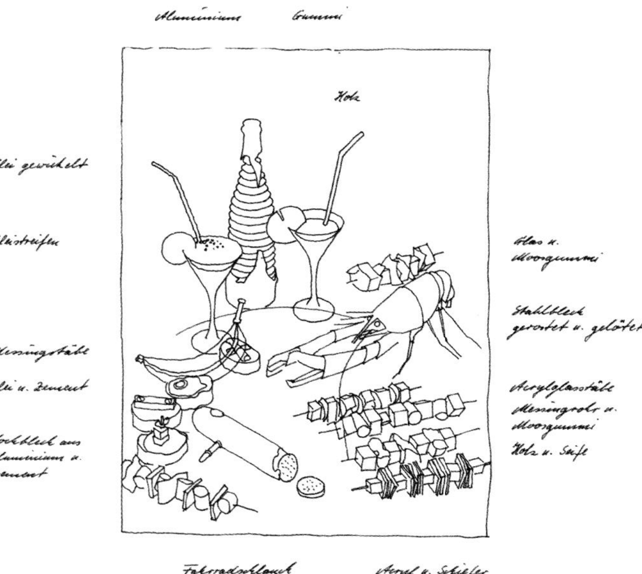

175

Student projects
Scale: 1:1,000
Photos: Gunter Lepkowski

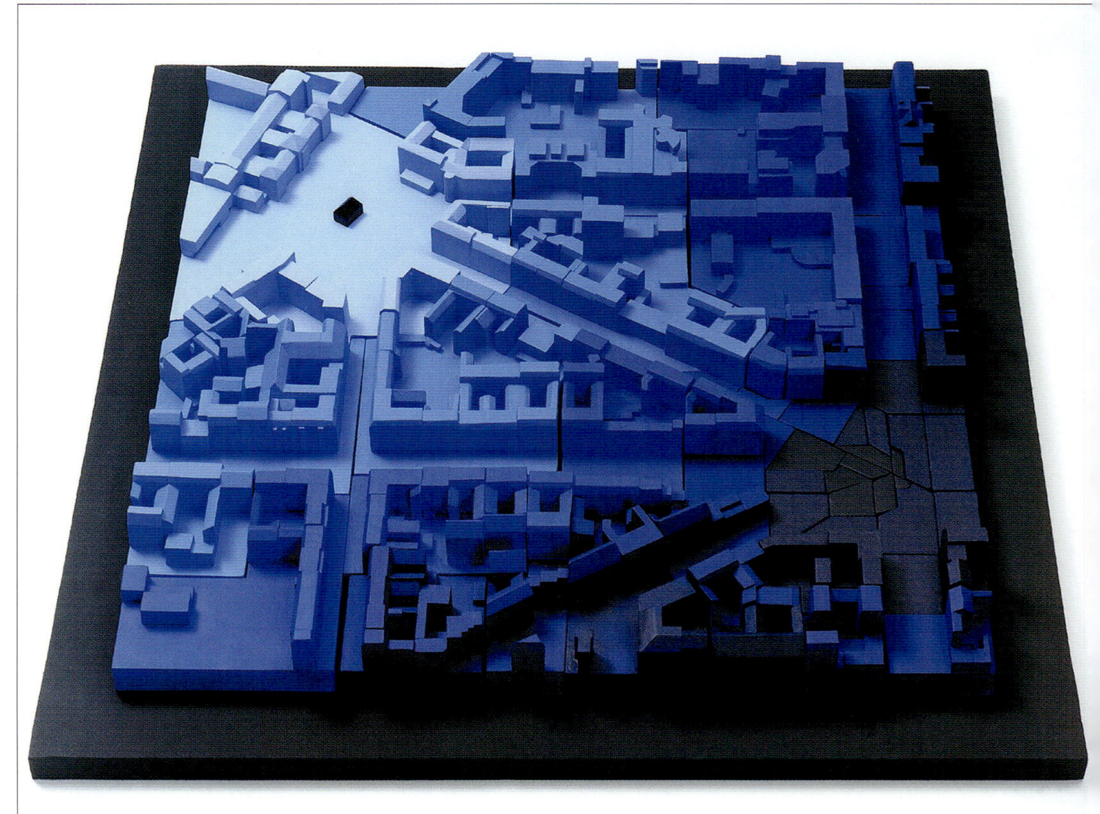

Student projects
Scale: 1:1,000
Photos: Gunter Lepkowski

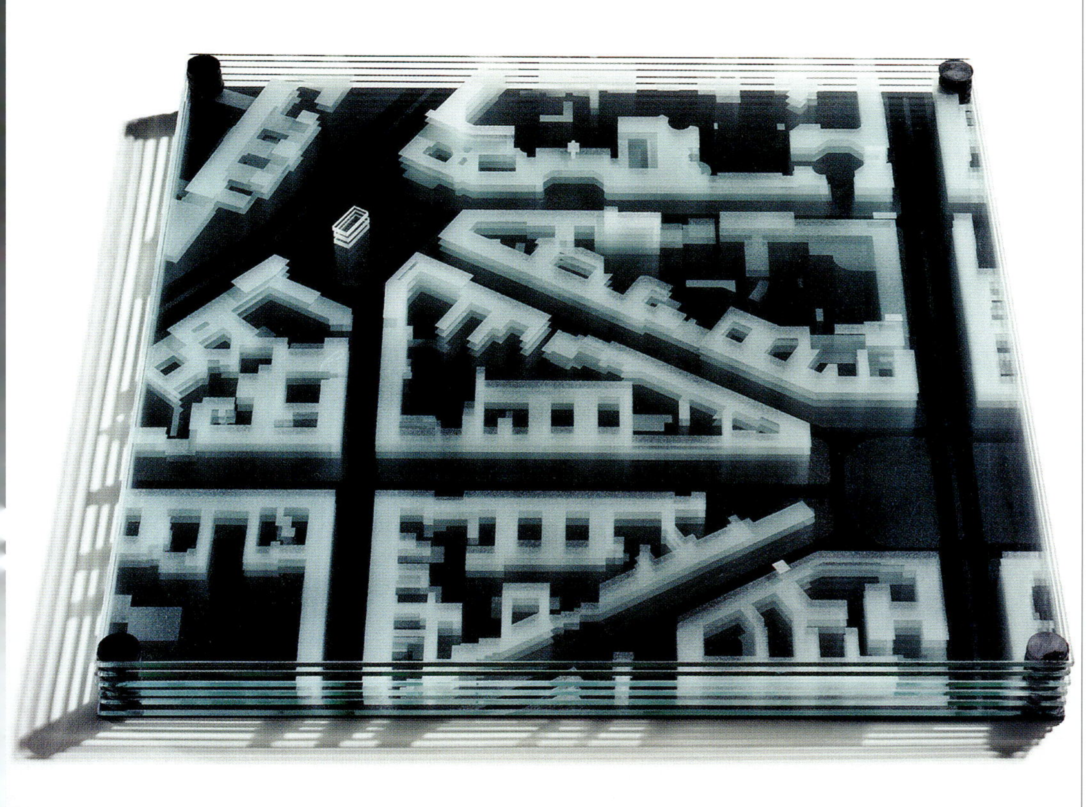

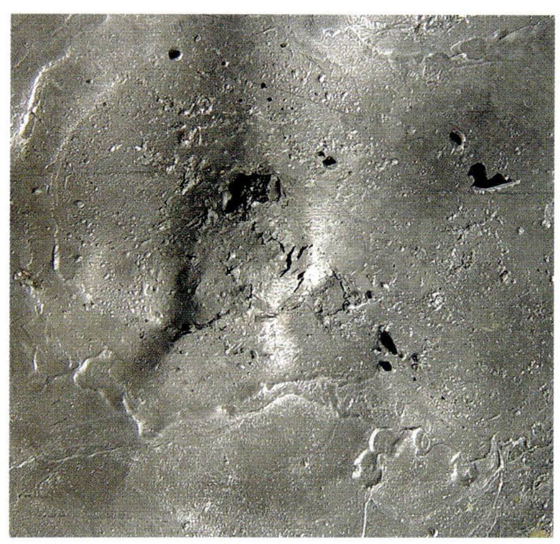

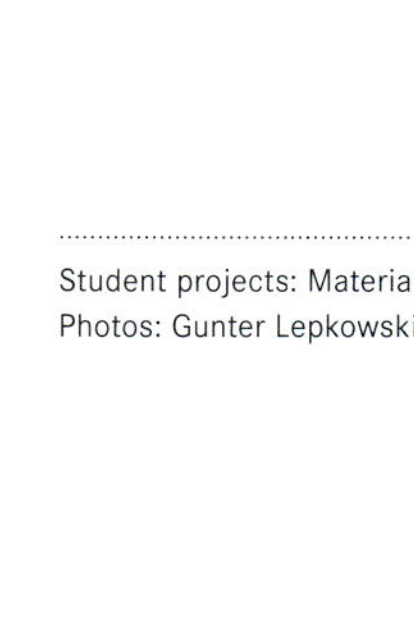

Student projects: Material studies
Photos: Gunter Lepkowski

01

01/02

Student projects
Scale: 1:100
Photos: Gunter Lepkowski

03

Student project
Spatial Interpretation of a two-dimensional art masterpiece
Roy Lichtenstein: Whaam!, 1963
Photo: Gunter Lepkowski, (c) VG Bild-Kunst, Bonn 2002

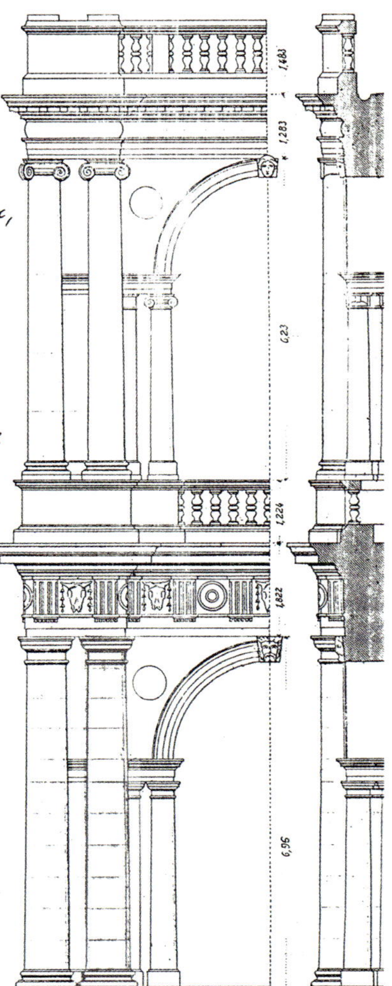

Student projects
Photos: Gunter Lepkowski

Helmut M. Lutsch
Berlin

www.a4-modellbau.de

Helmut M. Lutsch is the proprietor of atelier4-modellbau, the successor to the renowned Berlin model builder Hans Günter Zechert. Zechert's wide-ranging lifework extended from the 1960s until the turn of the millennium. He accompanied East Berlin's architectural and city-planning epochs before the change of power and all of Berlin afterwards. He built the large Berlin city model for the reunification of the city, in which utopian elements are found alongside realised ones. Since 2000 Helmut Lutsch has been running the studio, rich in tradition and now called atelier4-modellbau. New manufacturing methods and techniques which take today's computer-based designing into account have been added to the craft of model building. At atelier4-modellbau, computer generated designs are realised with CNC technology, and highly detailed models with skilled craftsmanship.

The technical work for an architectural model is always based on a plan. Photomontages can also serve as a basis, as they did for the *Wasserstadt Haveleck* development in Berlin and the *Alameda Park* in Mexico City. These virtual reality representations dictate the perspective in which the model is built. The method highlights the technical proximity between computer-generated images and the material representation of an architectural design. The actual model may be a product of computer technology, but it is nevertheless essential for presenting the fundamentals of an architectural idea. Leaving aside changeable aesthetic details, the model embodies the physical structure and the way parts relate to each other and to the surroundings, features that also determine the choice of material from a boundless variety ranging from stone, metals, wood and plaster to all kinds of plastics. Untreated woods as used in the *Wasserstadt Haveleck* models, for instance, are employed as a contrast to monochrome surface areas and volumes. Transparent buildings or fragments of buildings on smaller scales, in turn, such as the models for Mexico City or the Port of Hamburg, are executed in matt acrylic glass. Depending on the angle of view, inserted layers of colour give the entire volume a hue that makes the model stand out even more clearly against its surroundings and helps it acquire a physical dynamism of its own. The choice of materials is always a response to questions of transparency or solidity, while the scale determines the level of abstraction.

Berlin City Model, from 1991
Client: Senate Department for Urban Development, Berlin
Scale: 1:1,000
Material: Block material, timber products, emulsion paint
Construction: Modellbau Zechert
Photo: Pietro Savorelli

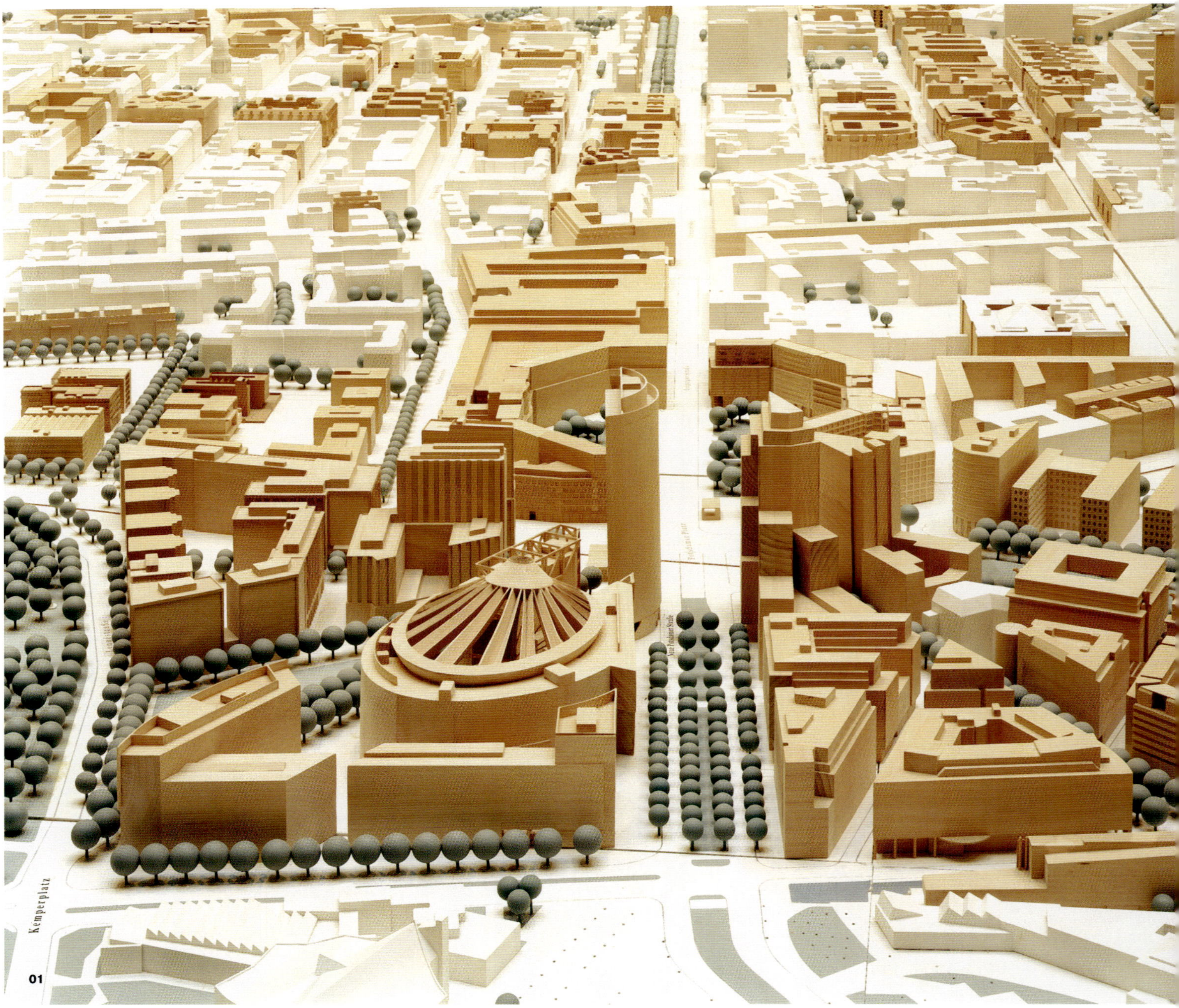

Kemperplatz
01
02

01

Potsdamer Platz, SONY Center, Berlin, 2001
Architect: Helmut Jahn
Scale: 1:500
Material: Pear wood, block material, emulsion paint
Construction: Modellbau Zechert
Photo: Pietro Savorelli

02

Berlin City Model, from 1991
Client: Senate Department for Urban
Development, Berlin
Scale: 1:1,000
Material: Block material, timber products
Emulsion paint
Construction: Modellbau Zechert
Photo: Pietro Savorelli

03/04

Wasserstadt GmbH Model of Haveleck, Berlin, 2000-01
Architect: Various, inter alia Baufrösche Kassel
Scale: 1:500
Material: Limewood, polystyrene, perspex,
emulsion paint
Construction: atelier4-modellbau
Photos: H. M. Lutsch

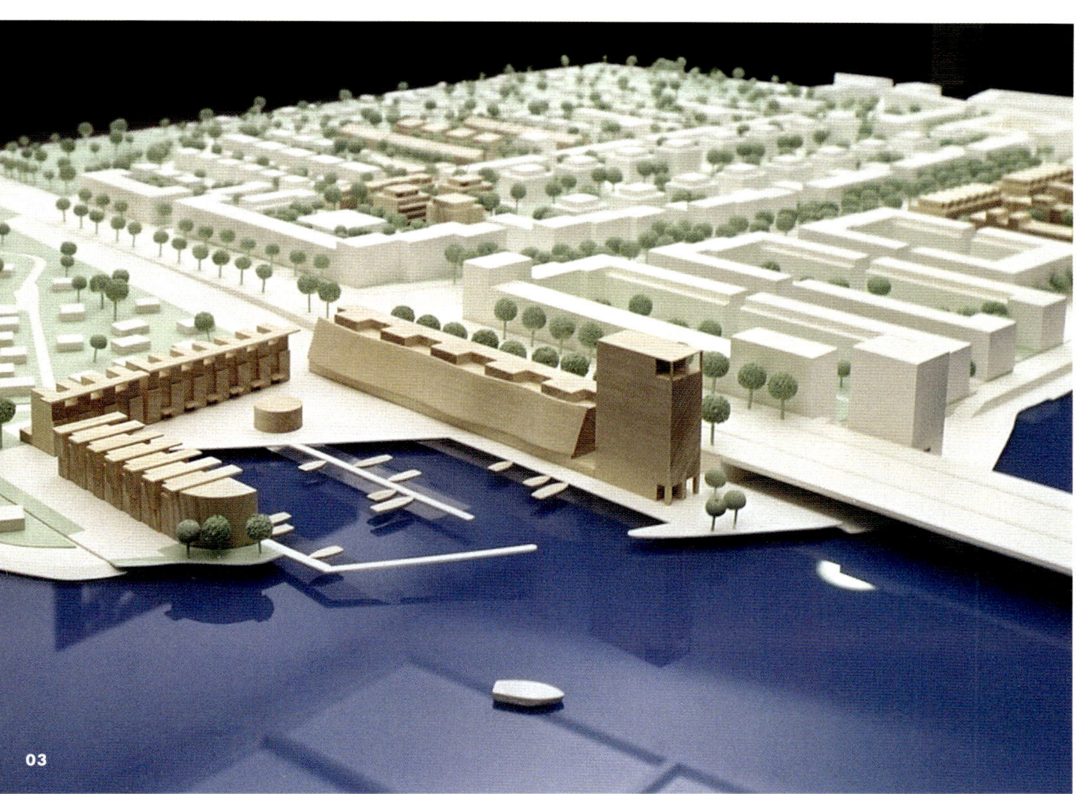

03

04

01

02

01 / 02 ....

Conversion of warehouse into media centre,
Hamburg, 2002
Architect: kaiserarchitektur.BERLIN
Scale: 1:500
Material: Perspex, pear wood veneer,
polystyrene, emulsion paint
Construction: atelier4-modellbau
Photos: H. M. Lutsch

03 / 04 ....

Schönefeld Airport Hangar, 2001
Architect: Blum und Partner
Scale: 1:100
Material: Brass sections, timber products, beech wood
Construction: atelier4-modellbau
Photos: H. M. Lutsch

01

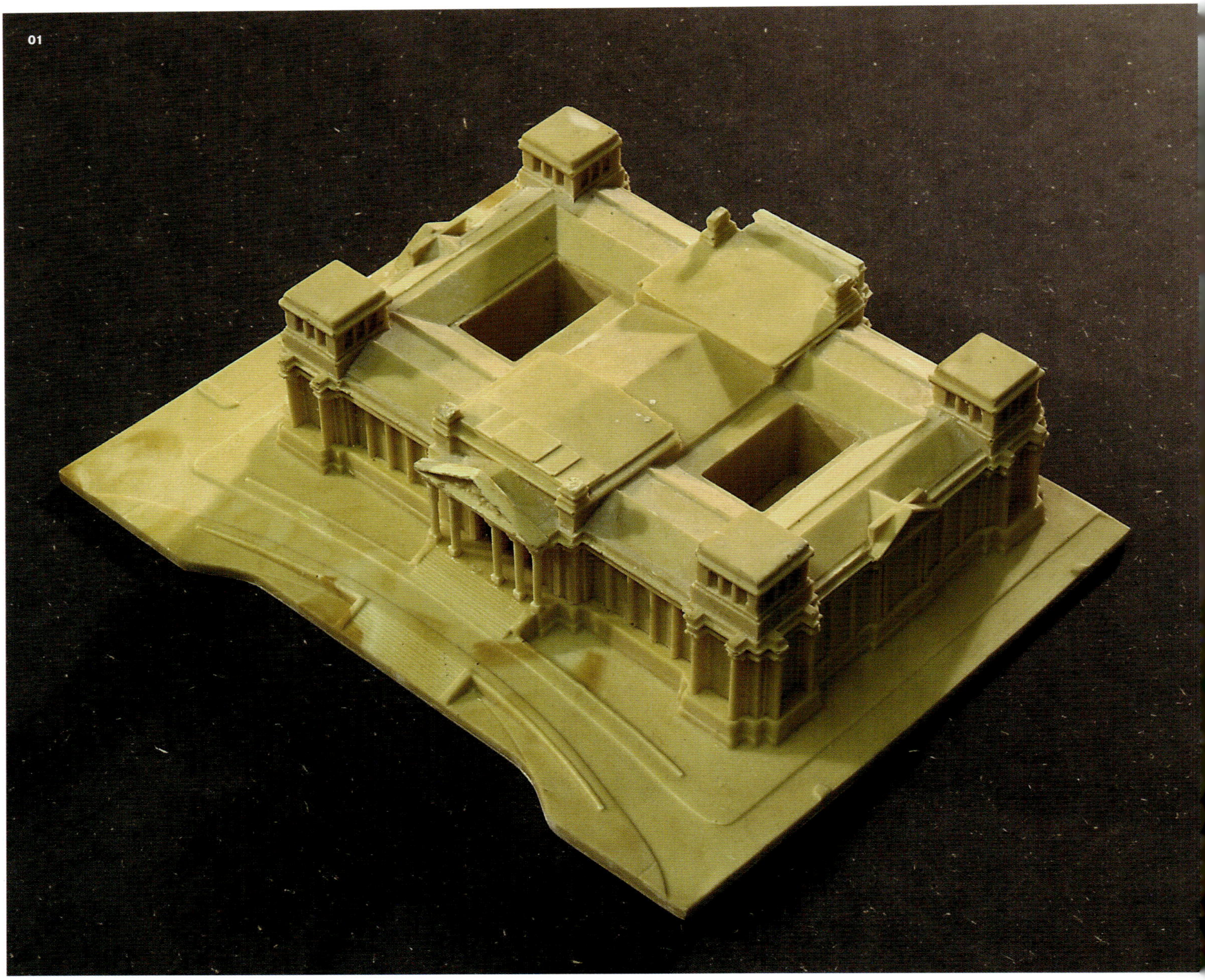

02

03

01

Reichstag model as a basis for competition
Client: Senate Department for Urban Development,
Berlin
Scale: 1:1,000
Material: Casting resin
Construction: Modellbau Zechert
Photo: Philipp Meuser

02

Workshops, Lorsch
Competition model, 2006
Architect: Numrich, Albrecht, Klumpp Architekten
Scale: 1:500
Material: Perspex, CNC-milled polystyrene,
coloured foil
Construction: atelier4-modellbau
Photo: Sartoris-Architekten, Bensheim

03

Wasserstadt GmbH Terrace Houses, Haveleck,
Berlin, 2001
Architect: Baufrösche Kassel,
Klaus Theo Brenner, Fink + Jocher
Scale: 1:50
Material: Polystyrene, precision perspex,
timber products, polyurethane foam,
natural materials, emulsion paint
Construction: atelier4-modellbau
Photo: Wasserstadt GmbH, Uwe Rau

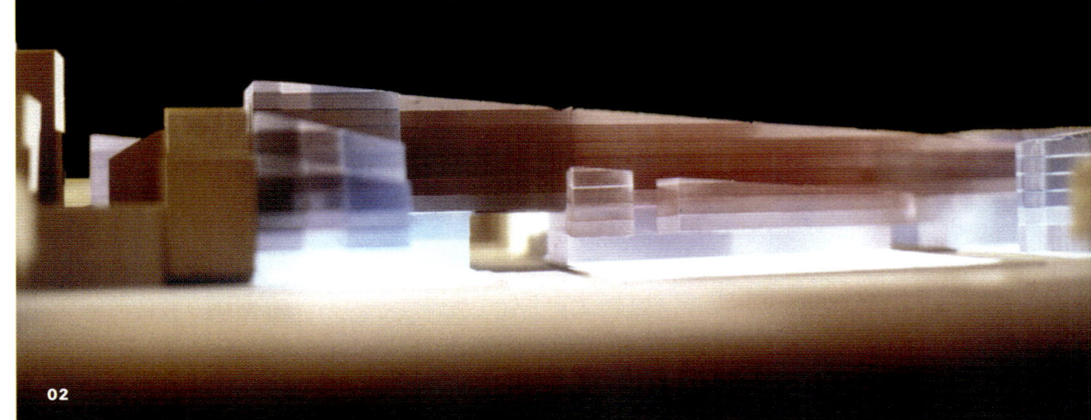

04

01 / 02 / 03 ....
Alameda Park, Mexico City, 1999
Architect: H. M. Lutsch
Scale: 1:500
Material: Coloured perspex, MDF, WDF
Construction: atelier4-modellbau
Photos: H. M. Lutsch

04 / 05 ....
Cemetery in the City
Architect: S. Knigge
Scale: 1:100
Material: Polystyrene, natural materials
Construction: atelier4-modellbau
Photos: Philipp Meuser

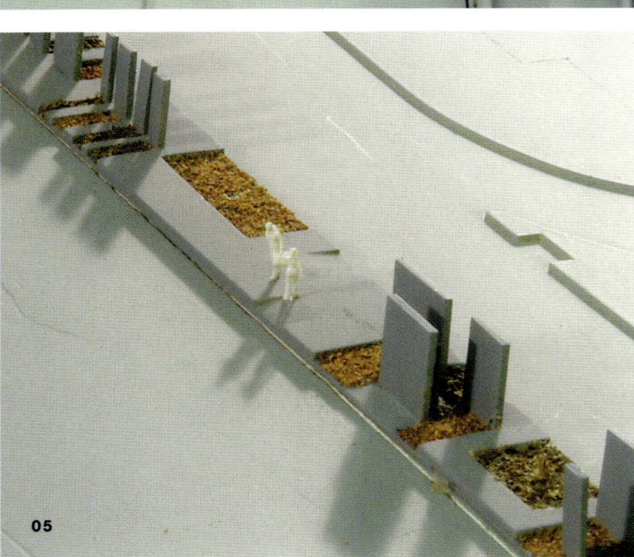

05

197

Julia Missner and Lars Lämmerhirt
Weimar

Extension/remodelling of the Anger Museum
in Erfurt, 2005
Architect: WPA Worschech & Partner Architekten, Erfurt
Scale: 1:100
Material: Pear wood, acrylic glass
Photo: Lars Lämmerhirt

www.modellwerk-weimar.de

When they set up modellwerk weimar in 2001, Julia Missner and Lars Lämmerhirt were still students of architecture at Weimar's Bauhaus University. Their first models, produced for architects' practices, were made of board and constructed at home in their apartment with the straightforward motive of financing their studies and their student life. The necessity that made model-makers of these two budding architects was mother to a company that is supplied both by architects and students with commissions.

They produce all manner of three-dimensional architectural models, ranging from urban planning models via section models to technical function models, training, orientation and competition models. Their varied fields of activity have an influence on their haptic model-making. For example, in the presentation model of the *Anger* Museum several varieties of representation converge. Their interdisciplinary approach tallies with the view that the model and the architect's design should be seen as a unit, and also with the aim of creating a functional synthesis of the arts. Beauty alone is not a quality criterion. A glance from the plan to the figural architecture and vice versa should open up immediate insights. modellwerk weimar's core concern is to produce models that make essential aspects as it were physically tangible for the eye, not merely illustrating the plans but arising out of them. For Missner and Lämmerhirt, pleasure in experimentation, the construction of partial sections to test the specific effect of materials, and alternative forms of expression – optically reduced or enlarged – are all part of designing demonstration architecture. This is also shown by their numerous project studies, some of which look so soundly built that one might think someone were going to move in tomorrow and live in them.

They work exclusively with top-quality materials. Along with accurate execution, contrast as a visual means is a distinctive feature of their models – wood and acrylic glass, white polystyrene, modules stained in discreet colours, various woods and light effects. In the case of colourless models, the impact comes from the precision work alone.

02

01/02/03 ....
Extension/remodelling of the Anger Museum
in Erfurt, 2005
Architect: WPA Worschech & Partner Architekten, Erfurt
Scale: 1:100
Material: Pear wood, acrylic glass
Photos: Lars Lämmerhirt

03

GHZ Munich Harlaching
Competition model 2005
Architect: worschech architects, Erfurt
Scale: 1:500
Material: Polystyrene (painted), acrylic glass (stained)
Photo: Julia Missner

01

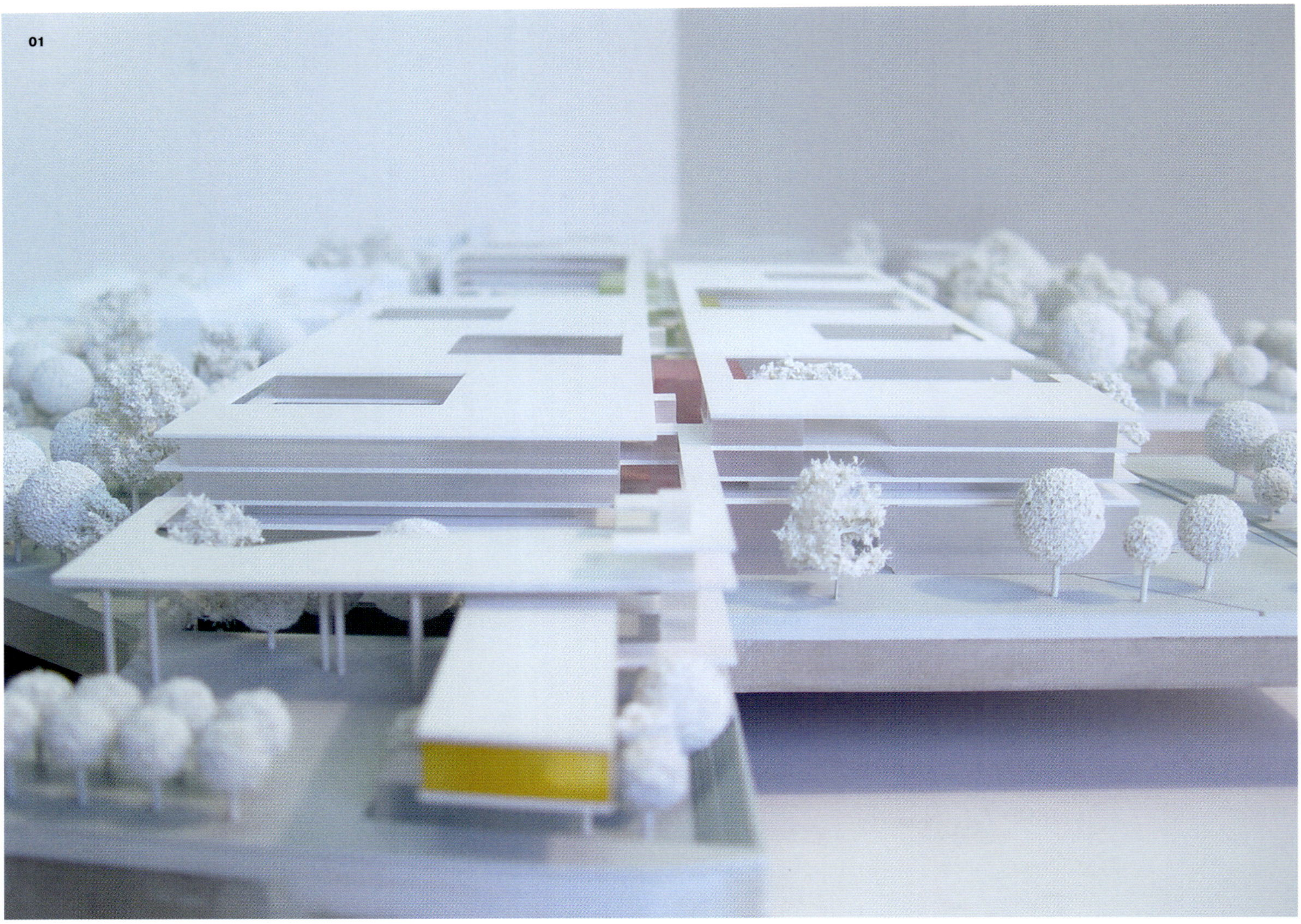

02

01 / 02

GHZ Munich Harlaching
Competition model 2005
Architect: worschech architects
Scale: 1:500
Material: Polystyrol (painted), acrylic glass (stained)
Photos: Julia Missner

03 / 04

Media & Print Factory, Bad Kreuznach
Presentation model 2006
Architect: Planungsbüro Ludwig, Weimar
Scale: 1:100
Material: Polystyrene (painted), acrylic glass
Model includes table and glass cover
Photos: Lars Lämmerhirt

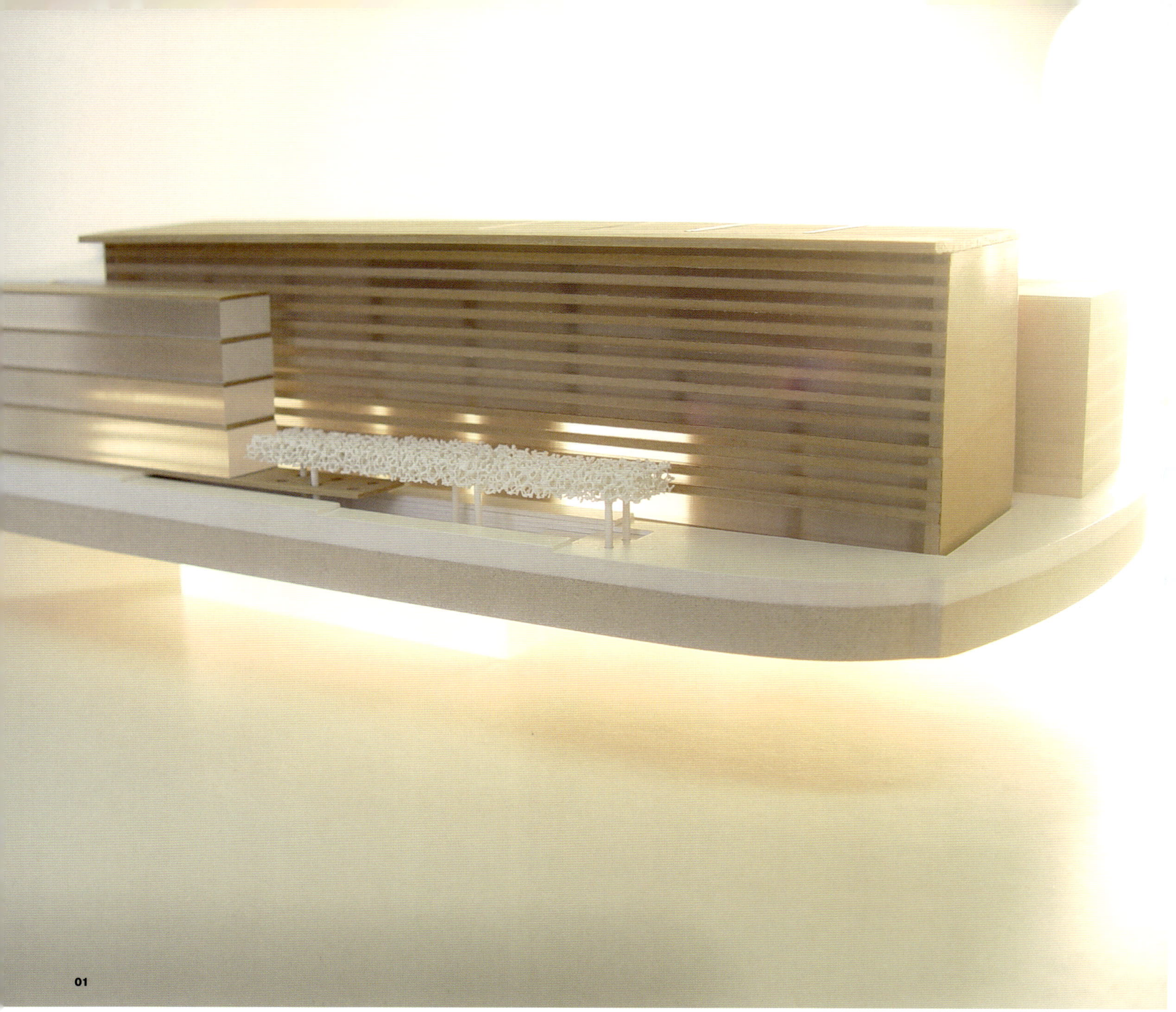

01

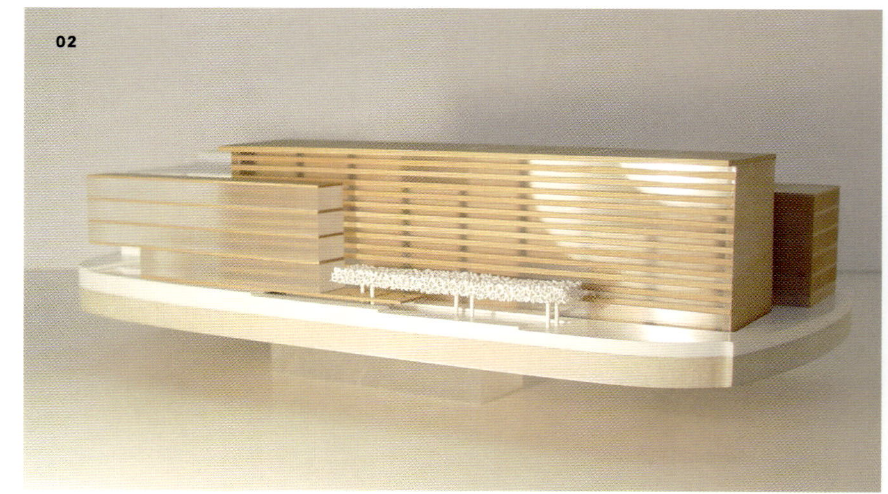
02

03

04

05

01/02

Landesmuseum Münster
Competition model 2005
Architect: worschech architects
Scale: 1:500
Material: Pear wood, polystyrene
Photos: Lars Lämmerhirt

03/04

Main Fire Station, Potsdam
Competition model 2004
Architect: Planungsgruppe Gestering, de Vries,
Wurster und Partner, Arch. J. Knipping
Scale: 1:500
Material: Polystyrene, pear wood ply (stained),
acrylic glass
Photos: Julia Missner

05

Pauritzer Strasse, Altenburg
Competition model 2004
Architect: Planungsgruppe Gestering, de Vries,
Wurster und Partner, Arch. J. Knipping
Scale: 1:200
Material: Pear wood ply, walnut (oiled)
Photo: Julia Missner

Christian Axel Monath and Klaus Menzel

Berlin

www.monath-menzel.de

The work of this company, established in 1985, is focused mainly on historical models, architectural competitions, presentation models in architecture and other fields, technical and scientific models and models for museums and institutions. Reconstruction models especially require something approaching to detective work, from researching plans and other documents through to analysing plan documentation and comparing photographic evidence. Even plan archives usually record intentions alone, and often enough one finds that people were still hard at work designing details while the shell of a building was already under construction. Moreover, when aiming to create a historical copy there is often a discrepancy between the original state of a building and its appearance after subsequent alterations. In that case, the replica in miniature always reflects a decision to opt for a particular date.

Meticulous work of this kind by Monath + Menzel has given rise to models for Berlin buildings such as the *Zeughaus* (Armoury), the Karstadt department store on Hermannplatz and the interior of the New Synagogue in Oranienburger Strasse.

This precision work is also evident in the competition and presentation models for current projects which represent the other main focus of this architectural model-making practice. Whereas the precision in a historical model lies in rendering a building exactly as it is or was, however, in the case of modern buildings the aim is to convey an idea that has yet to take shape. The competition model must not be a substitute for imagination, but presupposes its existence. In the competition segment, Monath + Menzel see the real art as achieving the right level of abstraction to generate the desired associations in the observer. Whether a model is more formalistic or shows the profile of the planned architecture in nuances depends on the client. Meanwhile, the form in which the conveyed idea is expressed results from the chosen material. A competition model is not a mere miniature, but gives form to a plan in order to stimulate the observer's imagination. Presentation models are an entirely different matter, however. The Berlin model-makers prefer to rely on style rather than realism to create such models' capacity to trigger impulses to buy the built architecture.

Persian Gulf Center Shiraz
Presentation model, 2005
Architect: von Gerkan, Marg und Partner
Scale: 1:500
Material: Pear wood and acrylic glass,
etched nickel silver sheets
Photo: Taufik Kenan

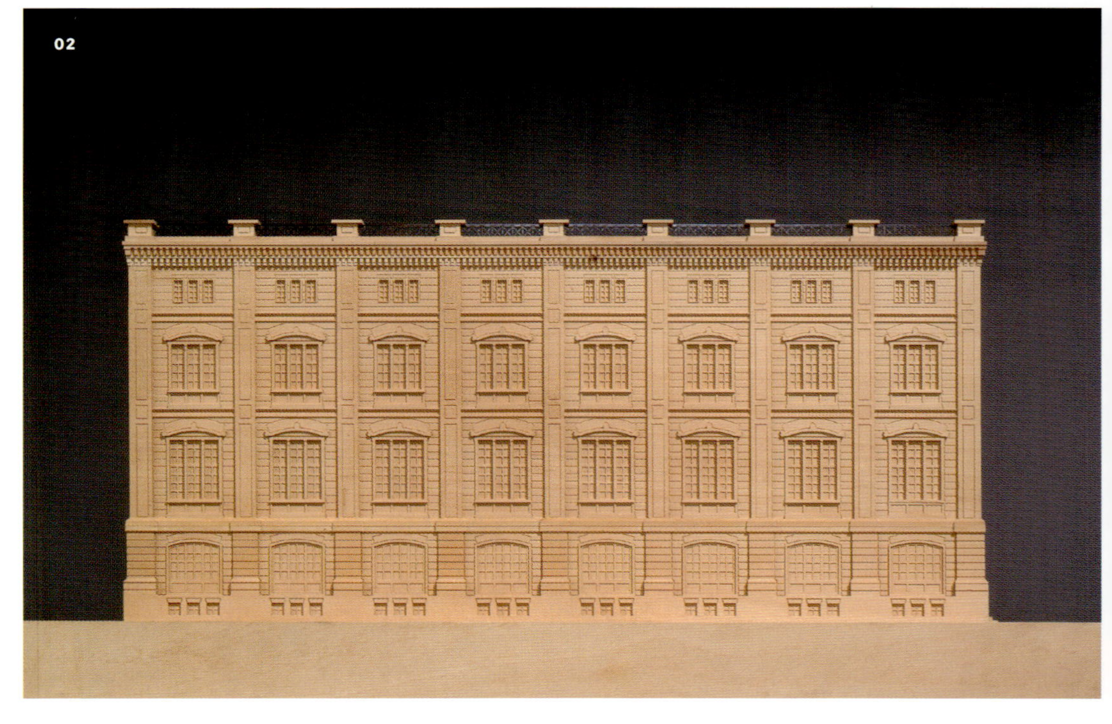

01

02

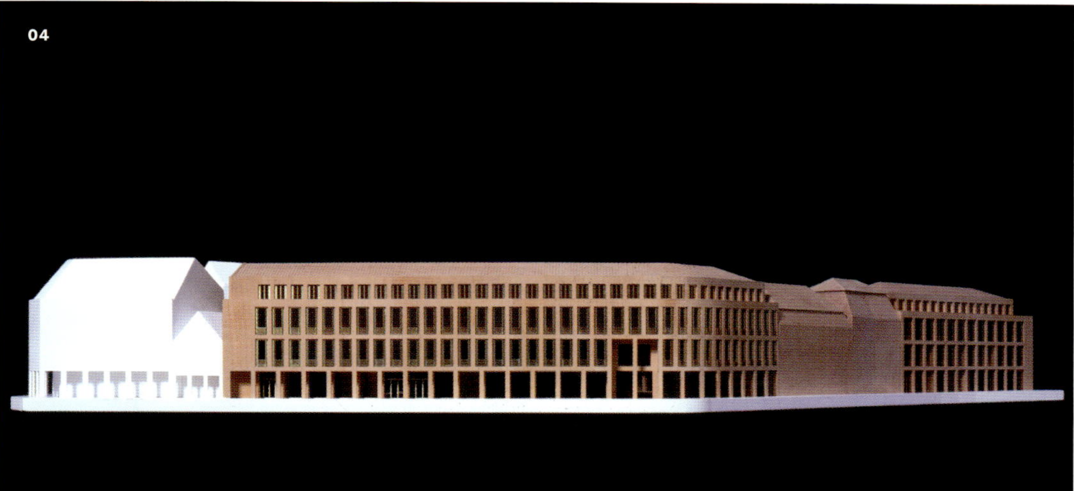

01

Staatsoper Unter den Linden, Berlin
Cutaway model, 2001
Architect: Gerhard Spangenberg
Scale: 1:100
Material: Beech wood, padouk, gold leaf
Photo: Antonia Weisse

02

Bauakademie Berlin
Model 1996
Own drawings prepared from
original sketches and dimensional drawings
Architect: Karl Friedrich Schinkel, 1836
Scale: 1:100
Material: Pear wood
Photo: Taufik Kenan

03

Foreign Office, Berlin
Presentation model 1998
Architect: Müller Reimann Architekten
Scale: 1:100
Material: Swiss pear wood, acrylic glass, brass
Photo: Ivan Nemec

04

Sparkassen Mall, Münster
Presentation model, 2000
Architect: Kleihues & Kleihues
Scale: 1:200
Material: Pear wood, brass
Photo: Taufik Kenan

05

Zürichhaus on Opernplatz, Frankfurt am Main,
Presentation model 2001
Architect: Christoph Mäckler
Scale: 1:250
Material: Pear wood, acrylic glass
Photo: Taufik Kenan

01

02

01

Interior of the New Synagogue, Berlin
Reconstruction from original drawings,
black and white photographs and hand-coloured
drawings, 1989–91
Architect: Eduard Knoblauch and
Friedrich August Stüler, 1866
Purpose: *Jüdische Lebenswelten*
(Patterns of Jewish Life) exhibition, 1991
Materials: Ornaments hand-made and reproduced,
hand-coloured
Photo: Gert Monath

02

Original drawing by Friedrich August Stüler

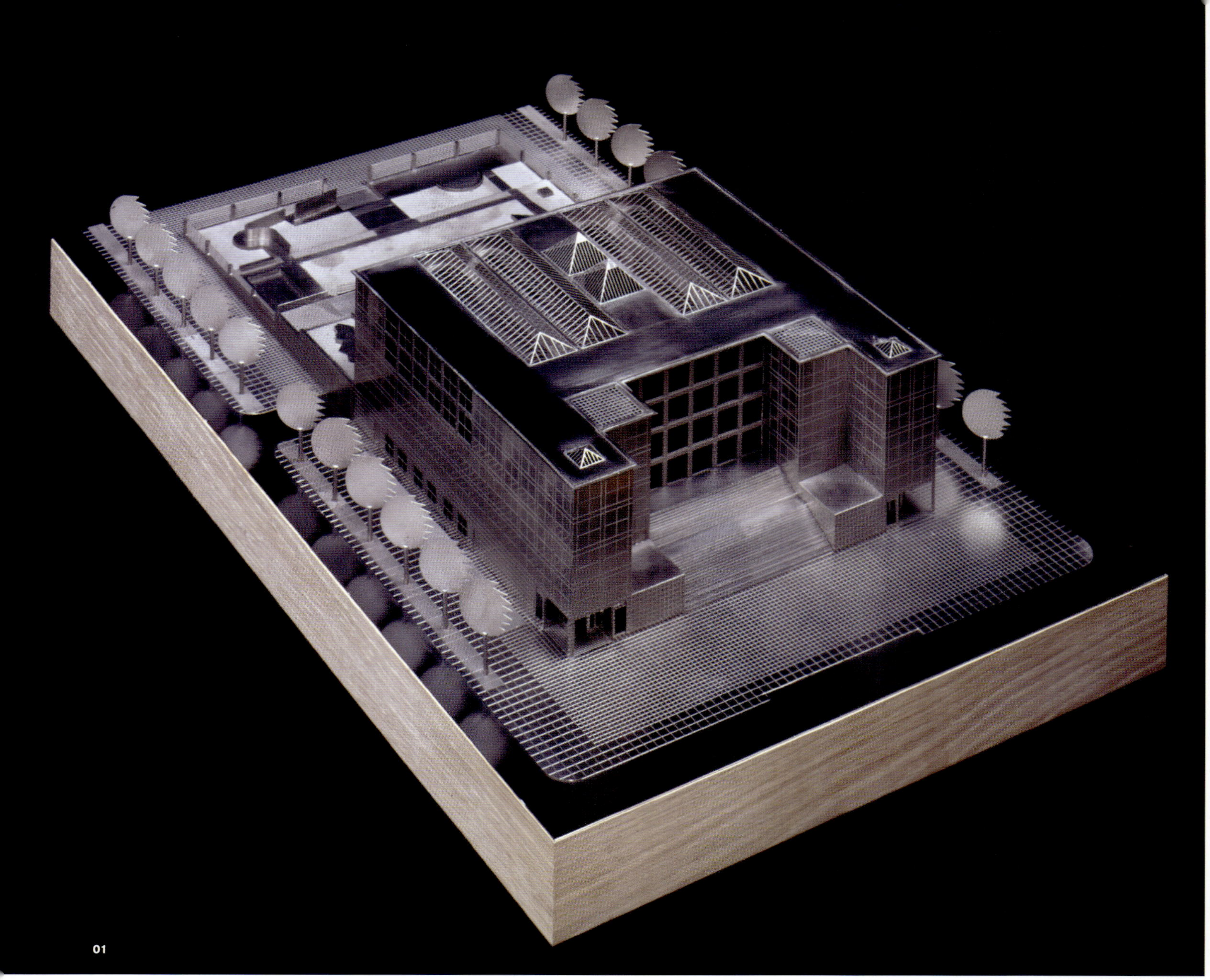

04

05

01

MCA Museum of Contemporary Art, Chicago
Presentation model c. 1990
Architect: Josef Paul Kleihues
Scale: 1:200
Material: Chrome-plated metal, oak
Photo: Gert Monath

02

Museumshöfe Berlin
Architect: Barkow Leibinger Architekten, 2005
Scale: 1:500
Material: Perspex, maple, CNC-milled bronze sheets
Photo: Axel Monath

03

Staatsbibliothek zu Berlin, archive building
Conceptual model
Architect: Volker Staab Architekten, 2005
Material: Ebony, aluminium, sepiolite,
painted insert plate
Photo: Axel Monath

04

Leipziger Platz 4, Berlin
Architect: Jan Kleihues
First prize in competition, March 1998
Scale 1:500
Material: Pear, nickel silver
Photo: Taufik Kenan

05

Federal Intelligence Service, Berlin
Architect: Jan Kleihues
First prize in competition, November 2004
Scale: 1:500
Material: Maple, nickel silver
Photo: Axel Monath

01

Rudolf Mosse Publishing House
post-conversion, Berlin
Architect: Erich Mendelsohn 1923 (conversion)
Purpose: *Berlin, Berlin* exhibition
Scale: 1:50
Material: Brass, hand-made originals of ornaments,
reproduced by casting
Photo: Gert Monath

02

Haus Liebermann and Haus Sommer
Pariser Platz, Berlin
Presentation model 1995
Architect: Josef Paul Kleihues
Scale: 1:200
Material: Swiss pear wood, silver
Photo: Frank Wölffing-Seelig

03 / 04

GSW Tower, Berlin
Presentation model 1990
Architect: Sauerbruch Hutton Architekten
Scale: 1:150
Material: Multi-colour painted plastic, sheet metal
(etched and chrome-plated)
Photos: Uwe Rau

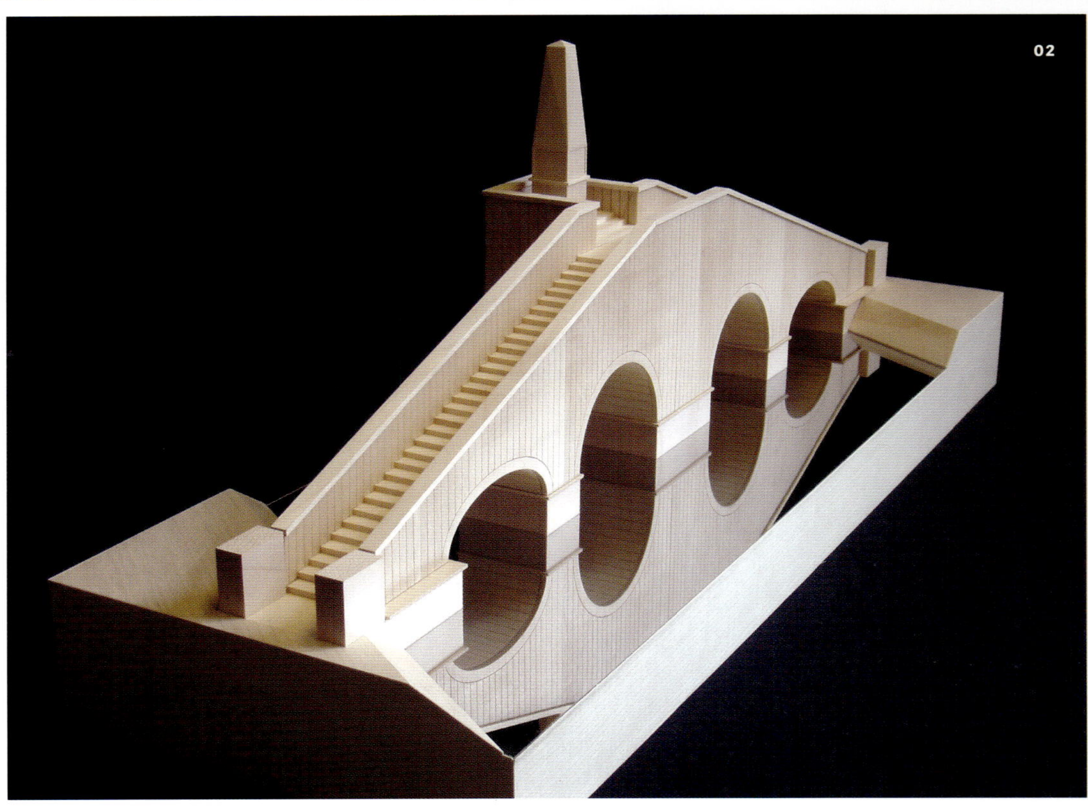

01

02

01 / 02 / 03 / 04

Bridges in the Schlosspark, Rheinsberg
Competition models 2004
Architect: Petra und Paul Kahlfeldt
Scale: 1:50
Material: Maple, nickel silver, stainless steel
Photos: Axel Monath

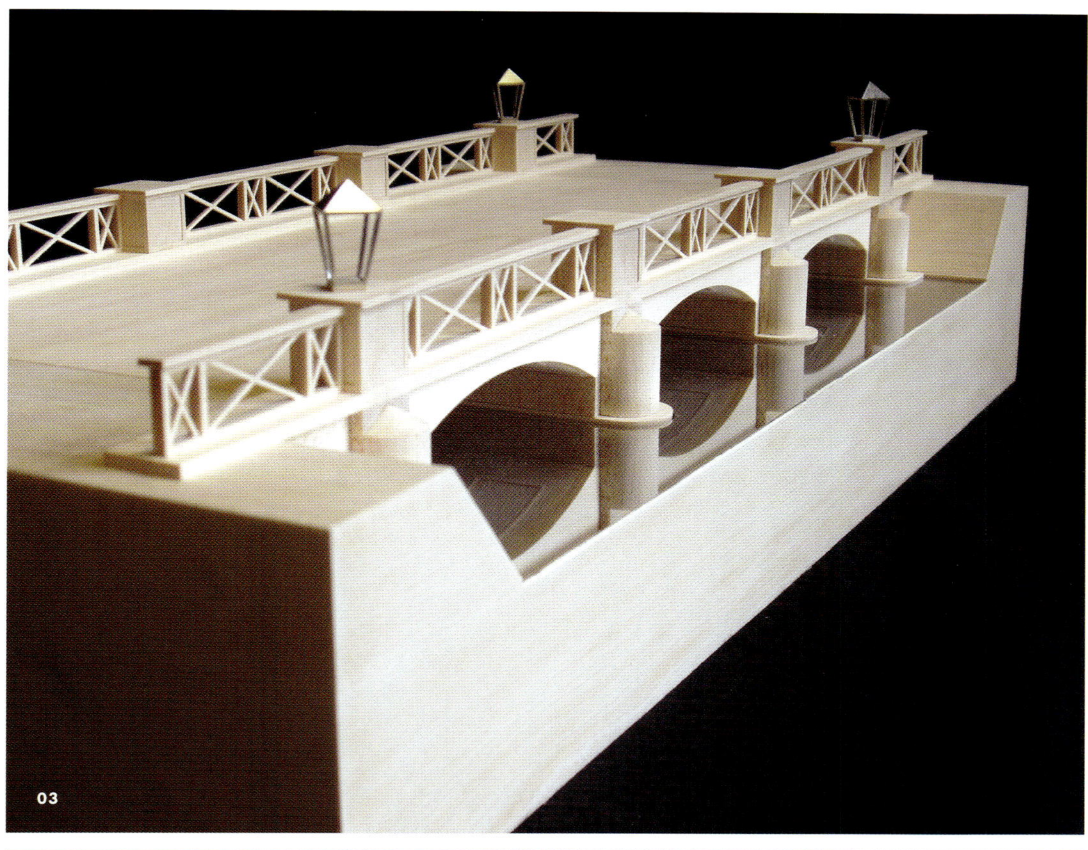

03

04

Gerhard Stocker

Vienna

www.modellwerkstatt.at

Models decide architectural competitions! Juries are confronted with the difficult task of choosing the best design among many concepts, and consequently many impressions, in a short time. Consequently, nothing is more important than an informative architectural model that enables a jury to grasp the core idea of a design and its key accents in a few glances. Model-maker Gerhard Stocker therefore considers the positions of windows and side entrances, the façade colour and other elements to be rather unimportant. Instead, he focuses on showing how a building fits into its surroundings, how it is accessed and what its function is, and on conveying whether the building or parts of it look light or heavy. He also considers it essential to show the interplay of architecture and green space planning.

His model workshop, established in 1992, accordingly relies on a clear formal vocabulary for competition models. Excessive detail is avoided, since experience shows that details change as planning progresses. The materials employed alternate between the sober, the coolly elegant and the decidedly colourful. In the case of town planning models like that of Vienna central station, colours and tints outline building contours, highlight elevations and underscore elongations. At first glance, the model could almost be mistaken for a virtual representation. In the case of the UNIQA, a hotel and office block by the Danube canal, play with the palette is focused on one building. Regardless of the choice of material or form of representation, Stocker's aim is to anchor the expressive impact that the new has on its surroundings in the visual memory and to stamp the design's core statement on the observer's consciousness. In the case of models with public appeal, the aim is to bring the general functional and aesthetic impact of the intended new building or buildings into a form that the eye can register in a single look. In models designed to promote sales, details are important. How are the doors and windows arranged? What materials are they made of? The model should answer these and other questions. It then exudes a feeling of living warmth, as for instance the Glanzing housing construction project does. A few accents suffice to captivate and impress – the white façades of new and old buildings, the loggias corresponding with the balconies, the widely branching red-tiled roof and the reddish-brown walls of the penthouses of these city mansions.

05

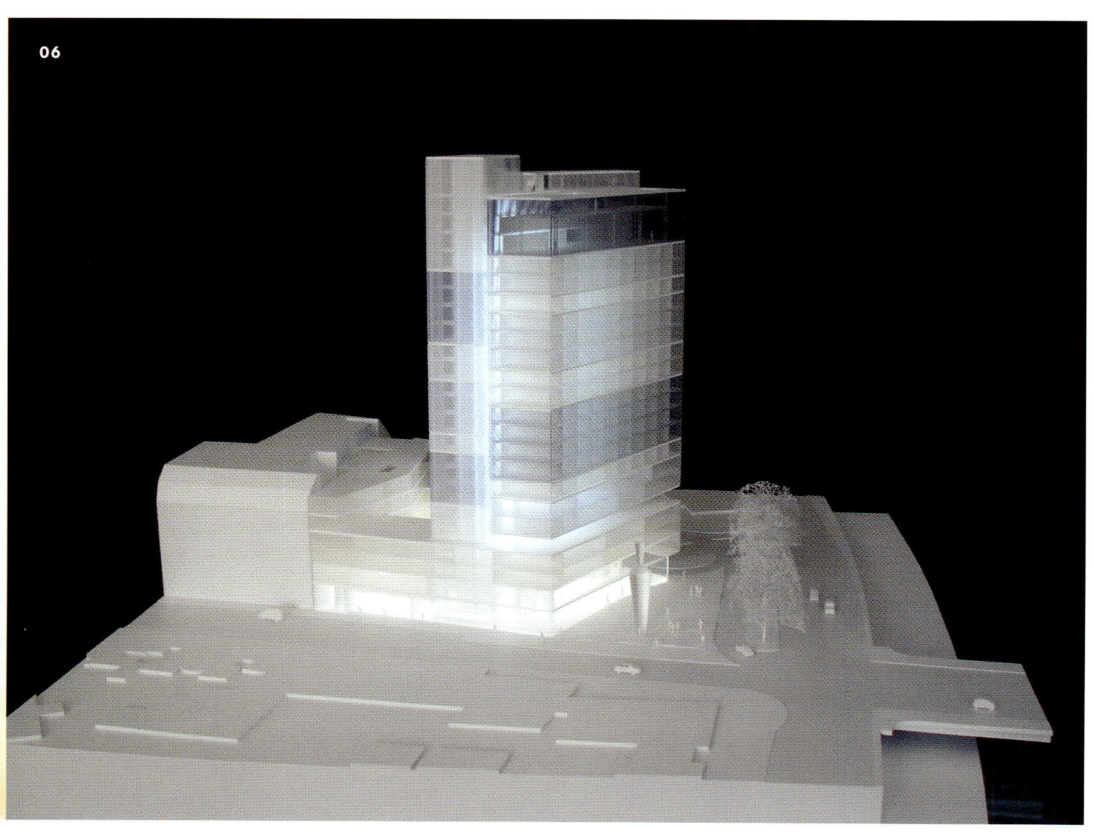

06

01/02

Höchstädtplatz, Vienna
Housing, first prize in competition
Architect: residential building (1): NFOG;
high-rise building: Raith, Gallister, Wimmer
Scale: 1:200
Material: Acrylic glass, screen-printing ink
Photos: Gerhard Stocker (1), Alfred Schmid (2)

03/04

Al Mutawaa Tower, Dubai
Architect: Dennis Lems, Söhne & Partner
Scale: 1:200
Material: Acrylic glass, screen-printing ink
Photos: Alexander Koller

05/06

UNIQA, hotel and commercial building
by the Danube canal, Vienna
Second prize in competition
Architect: Paul Katzberger
Scale: 1:200
Material: Acrylic glass, screen-printing ink
Photos: Gerhard Stocker

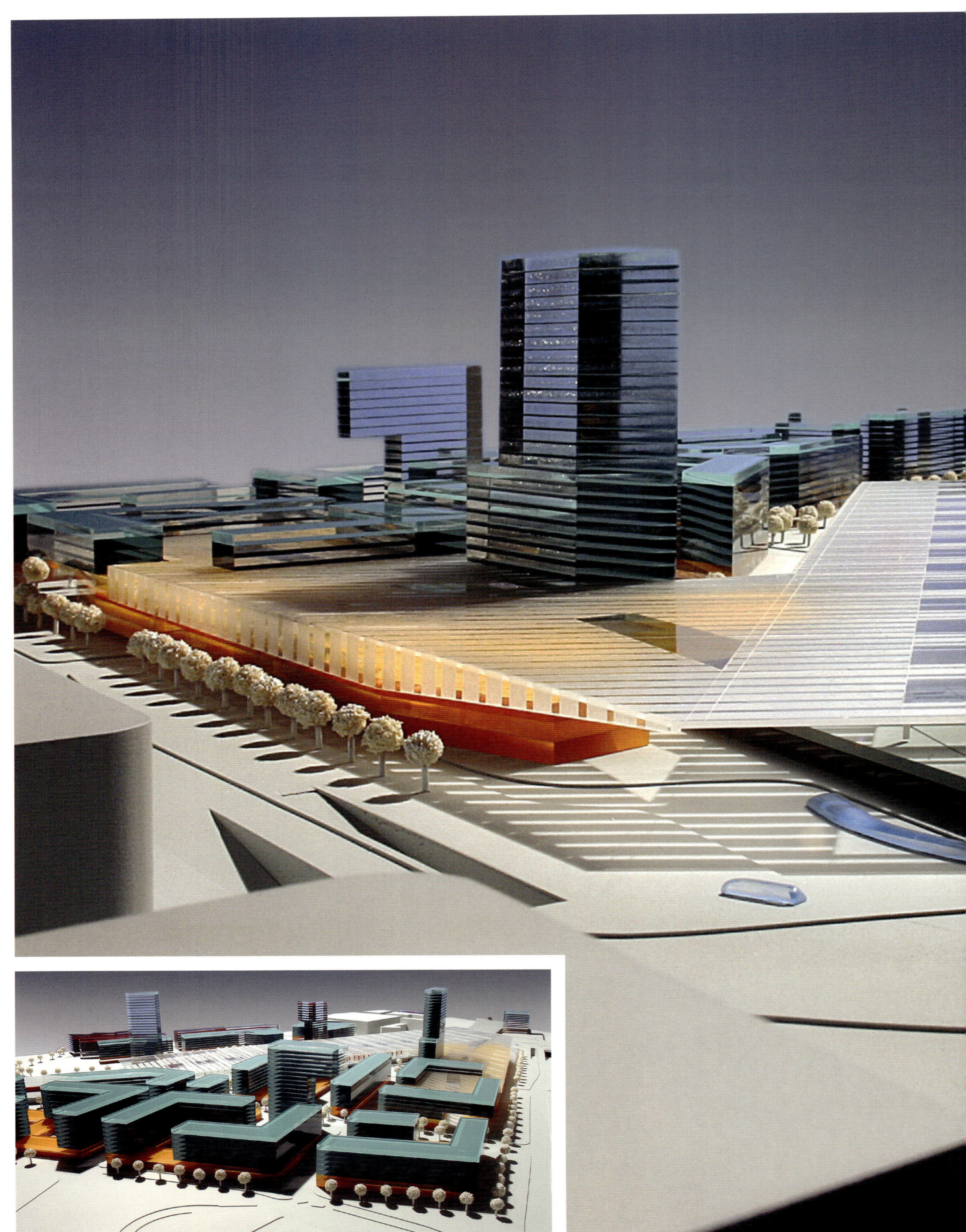

Vienna Central Station
First prize in urban development competition
Architect: Albert Wimmer
Scale: 1:1,000
Material: Acrylic glass, screen-printing ink
Photo: Alfred Schmid

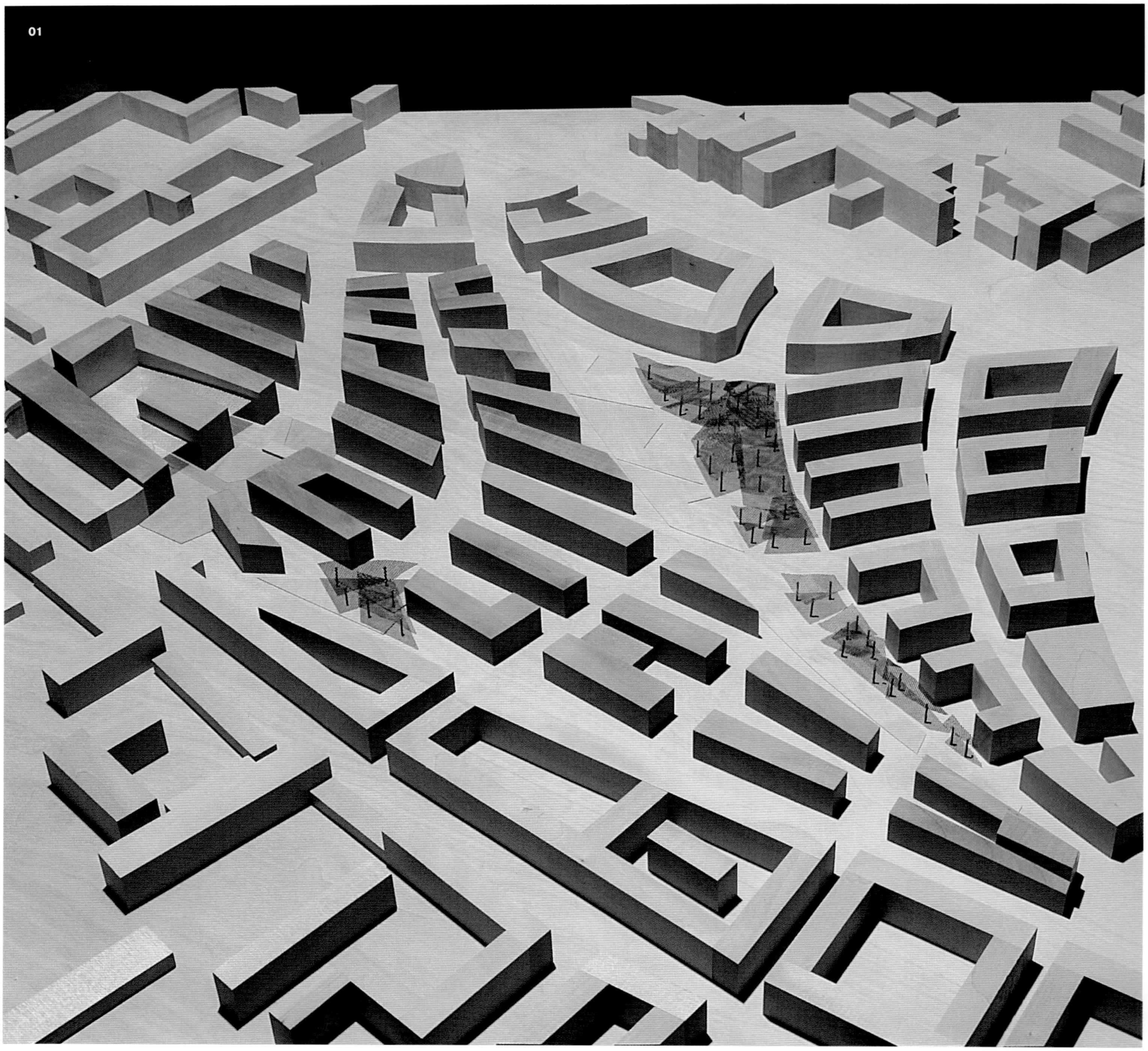

01

02

01

Eurogate Wien
First prize in urban development competition
Architect: Albert Wimmer
Scale: 1:1,000
Material: Pear wood, partly oiled
Photo: Alfred Schmid

02

Master Plan, Vienna Central Station
Client: Austrian Federal Railways (ÖBB)
Scale: 1:500
Material: Pear wood
Photo: Alfred Schmid

03 / 04 / 05

U2 Station, U2 Underground Line Extension, Vienna
Competition
Architects: AN_Architects
Scale: 1:200
Material: Acrylic glass, screen-printing ink
Photos: Herbert Schwingenschlögl

01

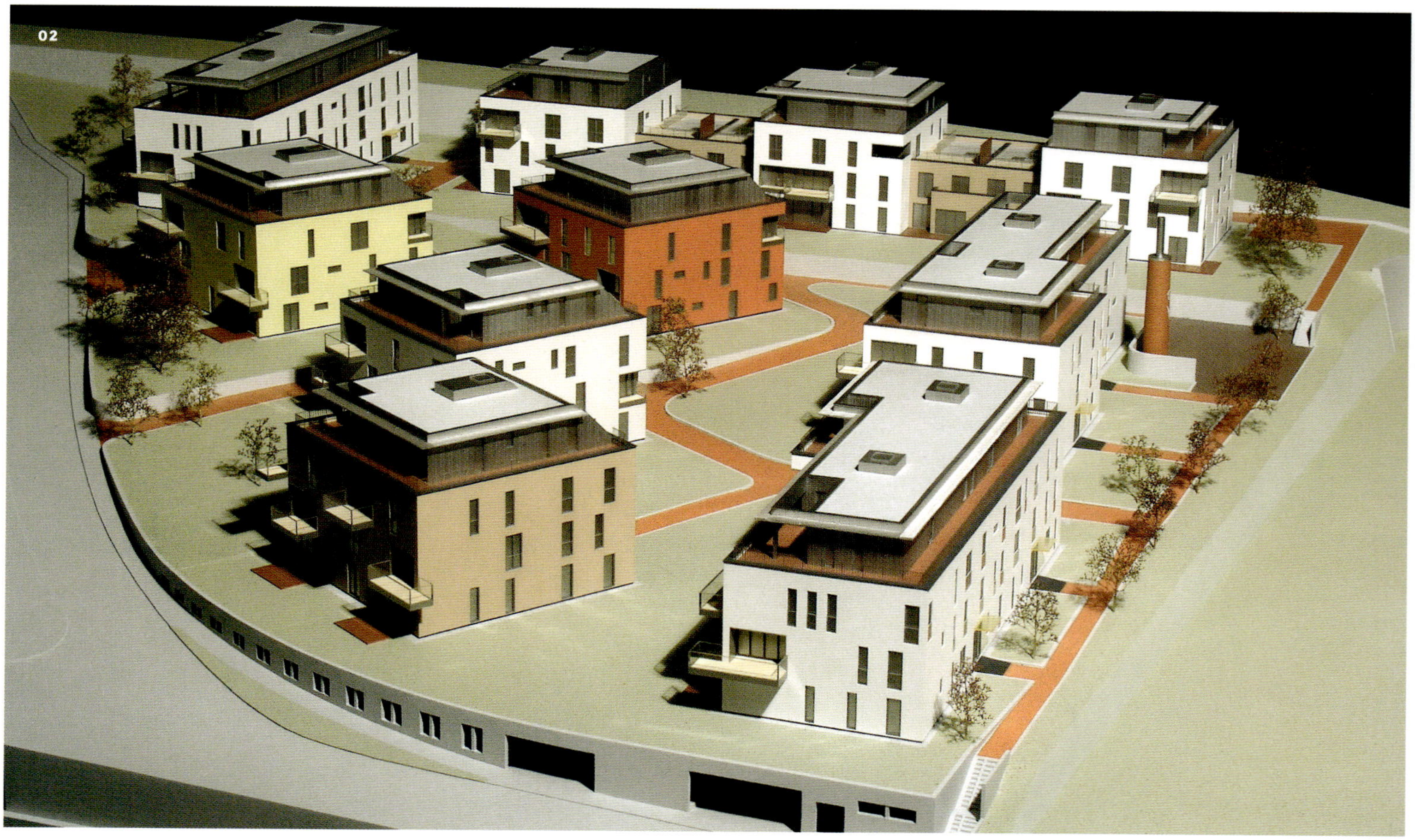

02

01 / 02

Housing on the Ölberg, Klosterneuburg
Client: Immorent
Architect: RCM
Scale: 1:100
Material: Acrylic glass, screen-printing ink
Photos: Gerhard Stocker

03 / 04

Apartment and Office Building, Seidengasse, Vienna
Developer: SEESTE
Architect: Ernst Maurer
Scale: 1:100
Materials: Acrylic glass, screen-printing ink
Photos: Gerhard Stocker

01

02

01 / 02 / 03 / 04 / 05

VIC-M, Conference Building Extension
Vienna International Centre
Architect: Albert Wimmer
Scale: 1:100 / 1:500 (competition model)
Material: Acrylic glass, screen-printing ink
Photos: Alfred Schmid

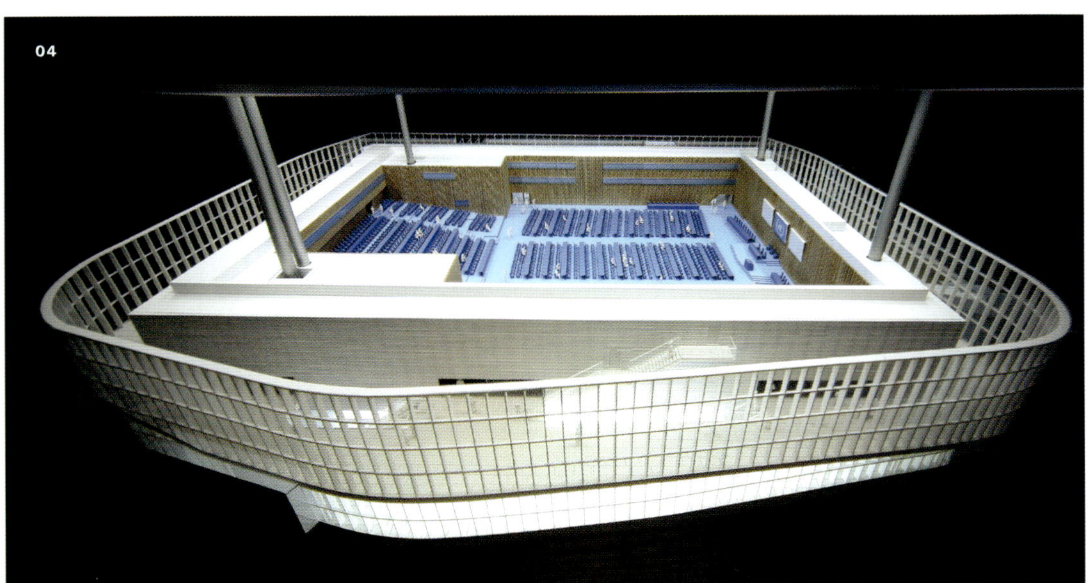

Gerhard Vana

Vienna

www.vana-architekten.at

01 / 02
Lower Saxony State Parliament, Hannover
Competition entry, 2002
External and internal view of the structural model
Architect: Vana-Architekten
Scale: 1:500
Material: Aluminium
Photos: Augustin Fischer (1), Vana-Architekten (2)

Vana-Architekten has run its own workshop since the mid-1980s. The Vana team does not see architectural models only as finished products that serve to illustrate architecture. Rather, they view the work of model-making as manual and mental in equal measure, as part of the design process. The practice's model-making workshop is therefore more a design workshop catering exclusively for its own requirements. Only in this way can Vana-Architekten integrate direct interaction between design and model into the work process.

The construction of a model is not necessarily preceded by plan outlines. Vana sees the creation of models as the heart of every architectural design strategy. These models are not necessarily only physical. The term *model* may relate to notional ideas, drawn depictions and CAD models as well as to the spatial and plastic embodiment of the design idea. Ultimately, any object could be illustrated by any other object if an appropriate relation could be constructed. For example, in the case of working models, everyday items are often, as it were, »misappropriated« and used as models for manipulation. The architects at Vana generally refer to design models when speaking of any type of model in the design process. Overall, they see these works as a series of model creations used to elaborate the conditions in which architecture can be implemented, and to concretise these conditions step by step.

Since relations can be reversed, every building may just as easily be viewed as a model of the design model. Accordingly, the Vana team sees implementation of the design model in the building as fundamentally a problem of presentation. Models and model operations that are used to execute the architectural design process are thus the essential artistic content that subsequently manifests itself in the built architecture.

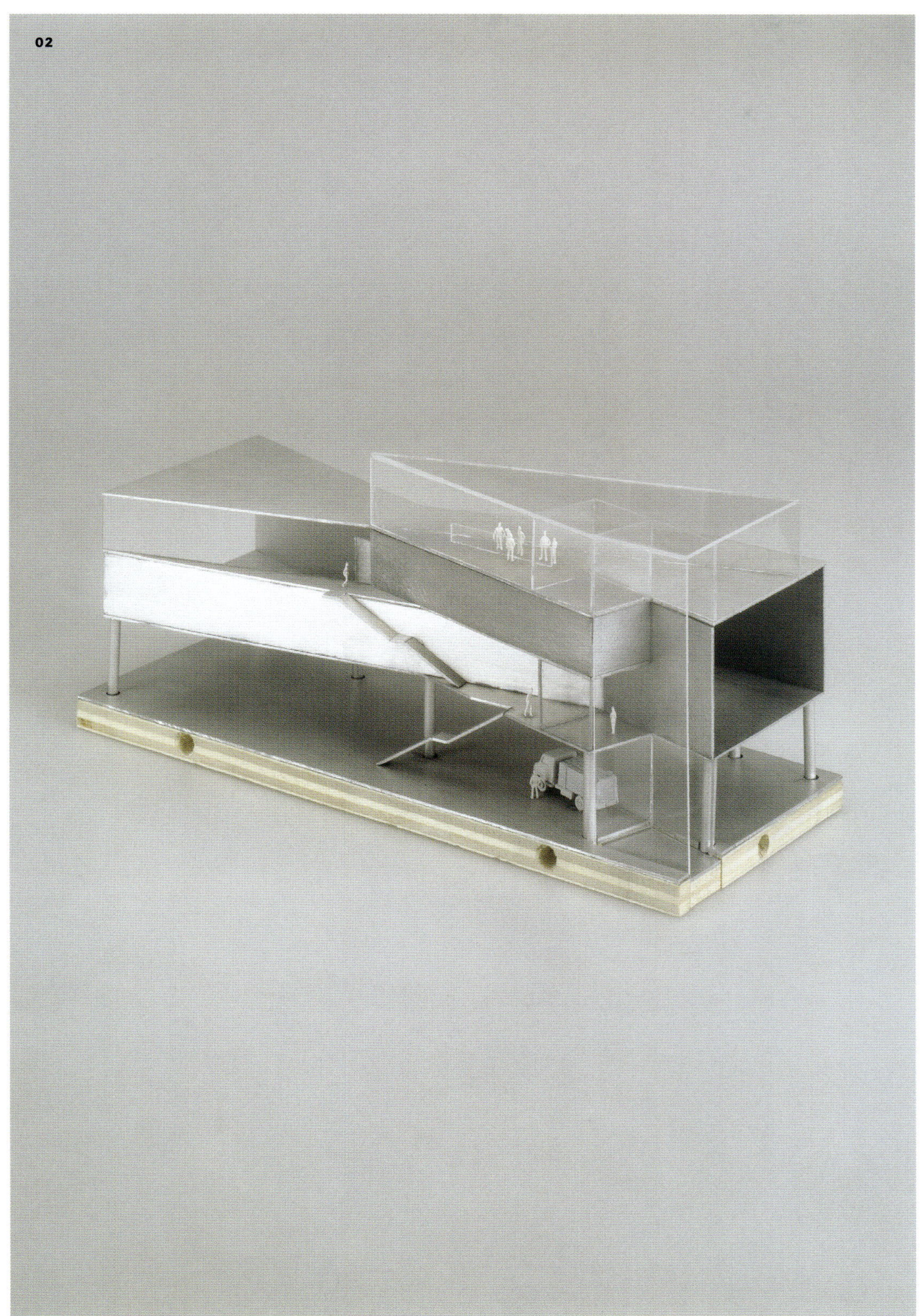

02

01
Art Repository for Franz Lesak
(based on a sculpture by the artist)
Project 2006
Architect: Vana-Architekten
Scale: 1:50
Material: Aluminium
Photo: Augustin Fischer

02
KHM Vienna, temporary exhibitions gallery
Competition entry, 2005
Structural model
Architect: Vana-Architekten
Scale: 1:500
Material: Aluminium
Photo: Augustin Fischer, Vana-Architekten

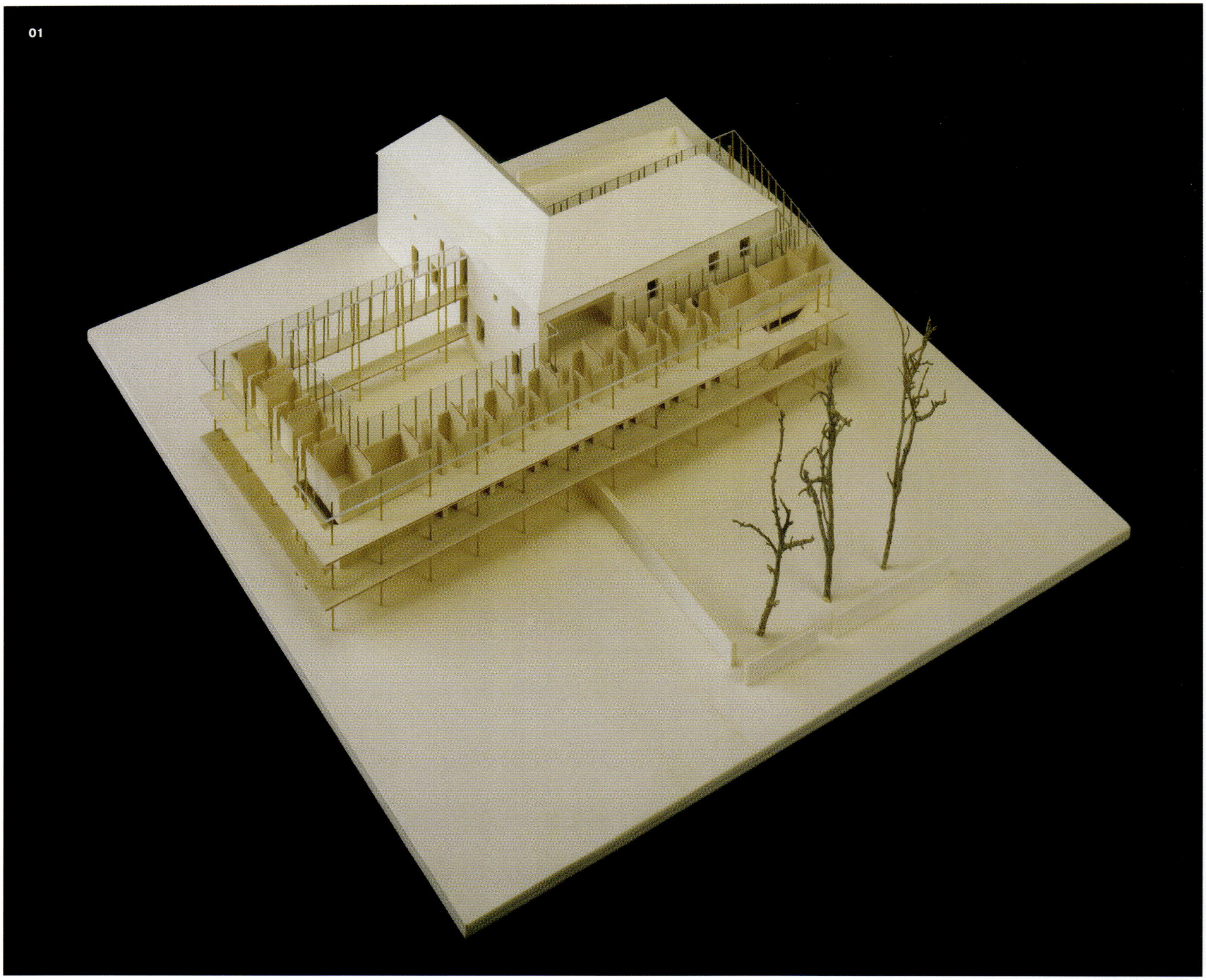

01

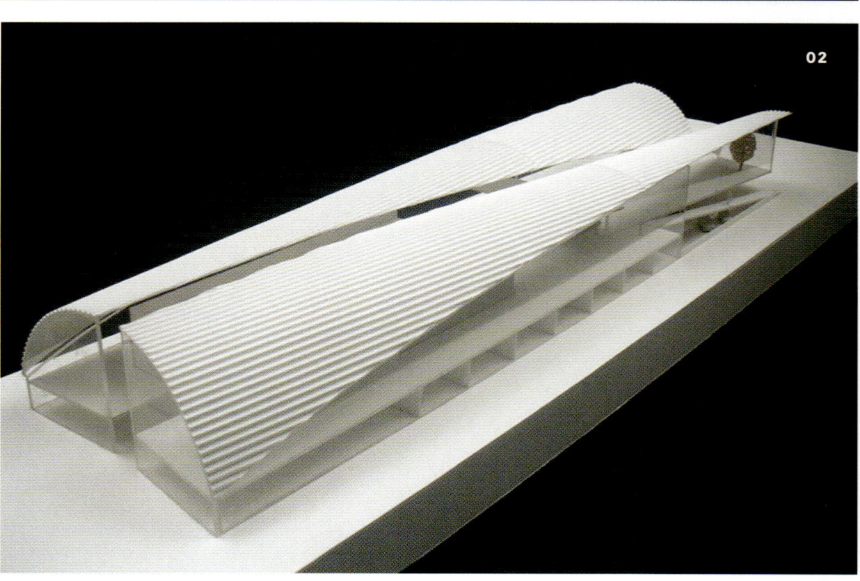

02

01

Living Museum, Dompierre-les-Ormes, France, 2002
Presentation model
Architect: Vana-Architekten
Scale: 1:100
Material: Wood, perspex, brass
Photo: Augustin Fischer

02 / 03 / 04

Vacation World, Stockerau, Austria, 1999
Working model
Architect: Vana-Architekten
Scale: 1:200
Material: Cardboard, perspex
Photos: Vana-Architekten (2, 4), Augustin Fischer (3)

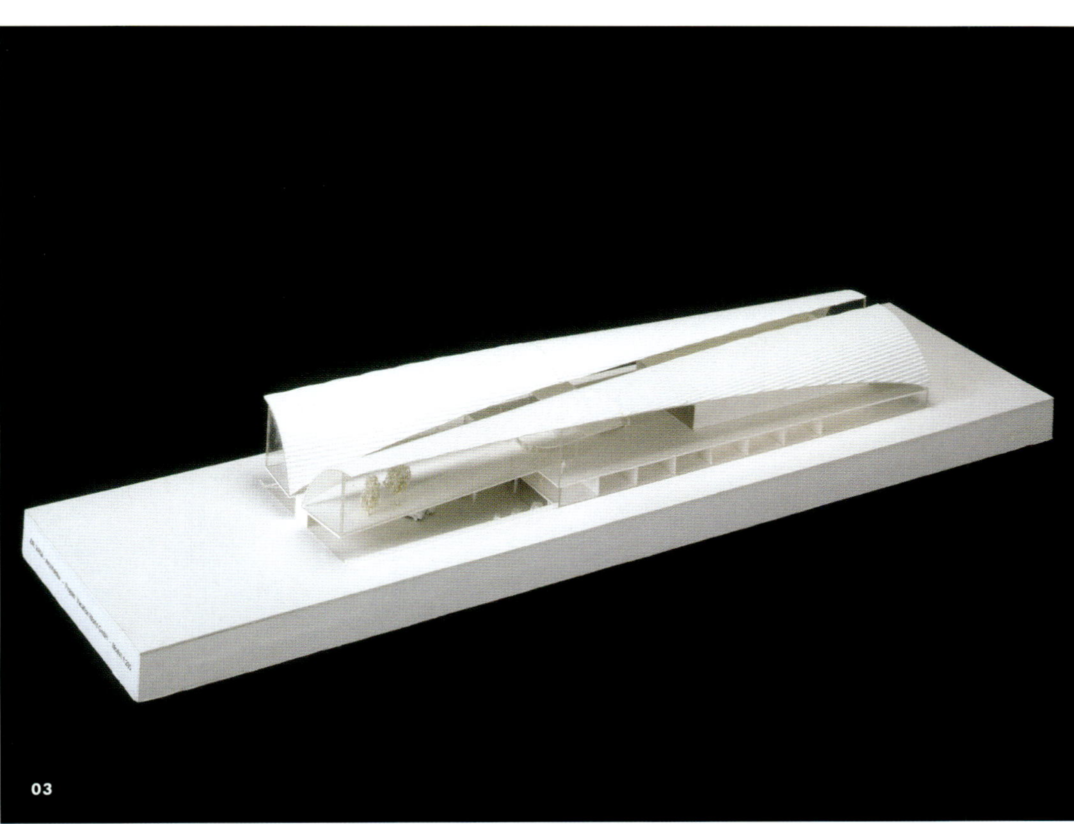

03

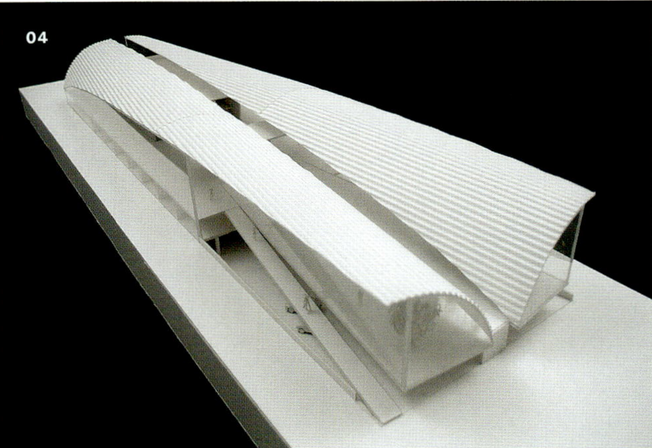

04

Christian Werner

Braunschweig

www.werner-modelle.de

Berlin Alexanderplatz
Test milling
Scale: 1:10,000
Material: Wild service tree wood (solid)
Photo: werner-modelle

Christian Werner made architectural models even as a student of architecture back in 1992. In those days, among other things he made competition models for well-known architects such as KSP Engel & Zimmermann at the clients' own offices. Since 1994 he has run his own workshop with a small group of colleagues. In the year 2000 the firm began making larger models for gmp architects, among them the 1:20,000 scale model of Lingang Harbour City that Meinhard von Gerkan took to China by aeroplane.

As a career changer and border crosser in architectural model-making, the company, which works mainly for town planning architects, entered new territory in making miniature townscapes and has taken the lead in filling a gap in the market. Since the Lingang commission, the demand for miniature model townscapes has grown steadily. As the role of the model as a way of translating an idea in a broad context was becoming more and more important, in 2005 the company set up scopulus®, a branch that specialises in georeliefs and model townscapes. Sometimes the two divisions are creatively interdependent and base their work on complex data processing that only a team of equals can deliver. A physics graduate from the Institute for Computer Graphics at Braunschweig Technical University writes the special software, a geology graduate finds and repairs the files, because a machined 3D model shows up every mistake, while another partner takes care of advertising and sales. Christian Werner himself manages the creative process of model production. His architectural models are aimed at abstracting reality and directing the visual message to the core design idea. The town planning models especially are sections of landscape that render the geographical and spatial references of building plans comprehensible. Some are made of wood, others of different, ever-new materials, since visualisation calls for new forms of expression from case to case. Regardless or maybe precisely because of that, these miniature models that allow people to experience the big picture look from a distance like relief carvings by the hand of a master woodcarver, from the patterns of which the design idea can be read.

Lingang, China
Competition model 2002, first prize
Architect: Meinhard von Gerkan
Scale: 1:20,000
Material: Wild service tree wood (solid)
Photo: LEISKA

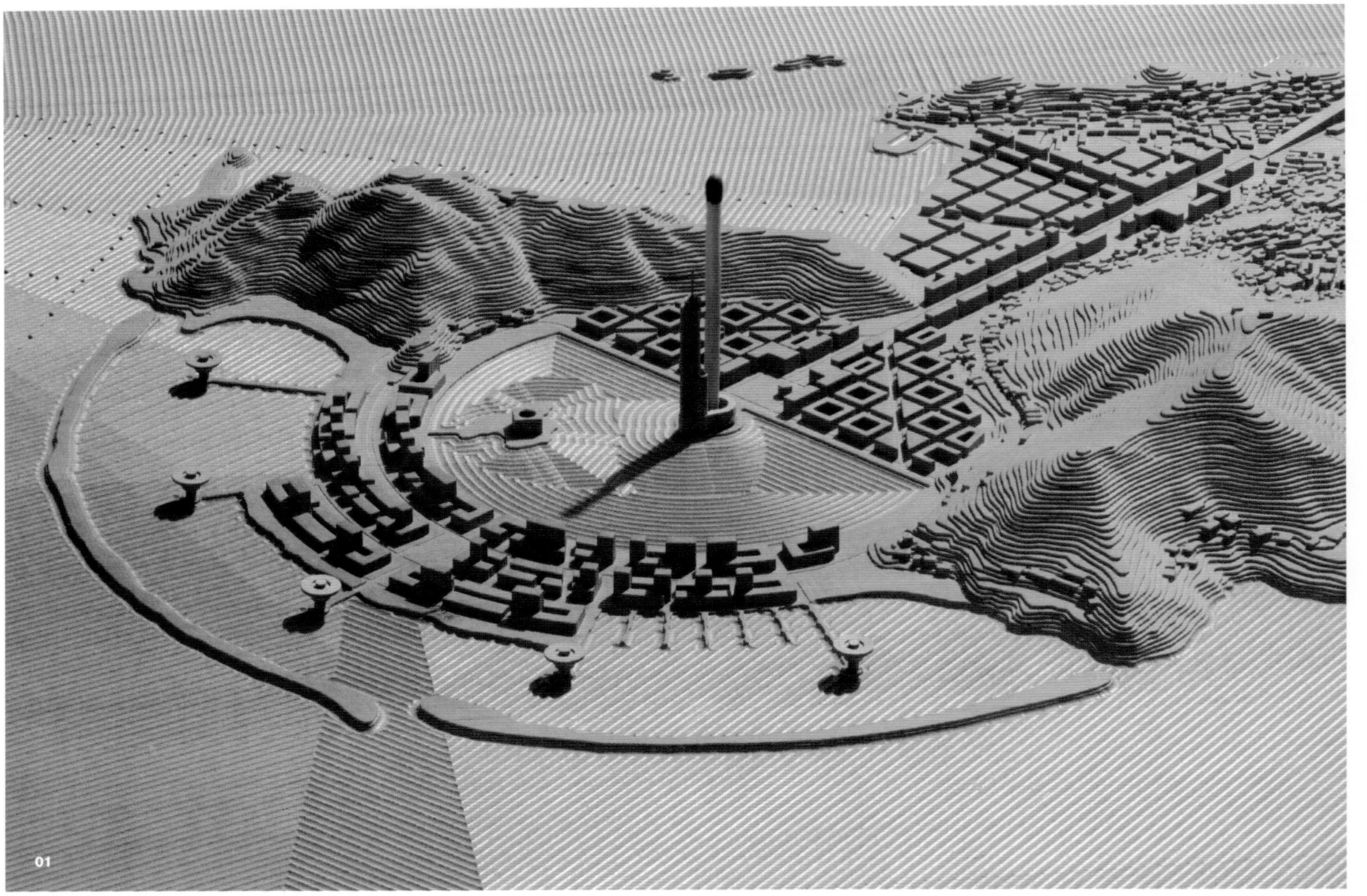

03

01/02 ....

Yang Shang Island, China
Competition model, 2001
Architect: gmp, von Gerkan, Marg und Partner
Scale: 1:10,000
Material: Wild service tree wood (solid)
Photos: LEISKA

03/04/05 ....

HafenCity, Hamburg
Presentation model for the Office of the
Federal State of Hamburg in Berlin
Client: HafenCity GmbH
Scale: 1:2,000
Material: Wild service tree wood (solid),
water surfaces stained
Photos: werner-modelle

04

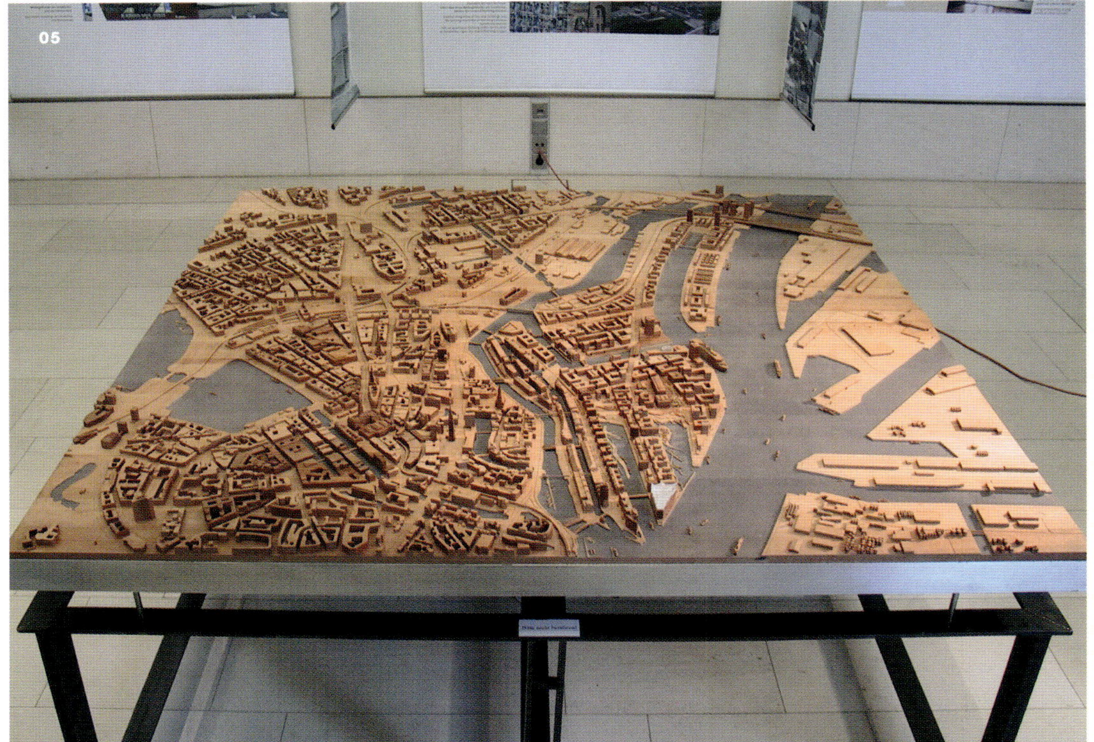

05

01
02

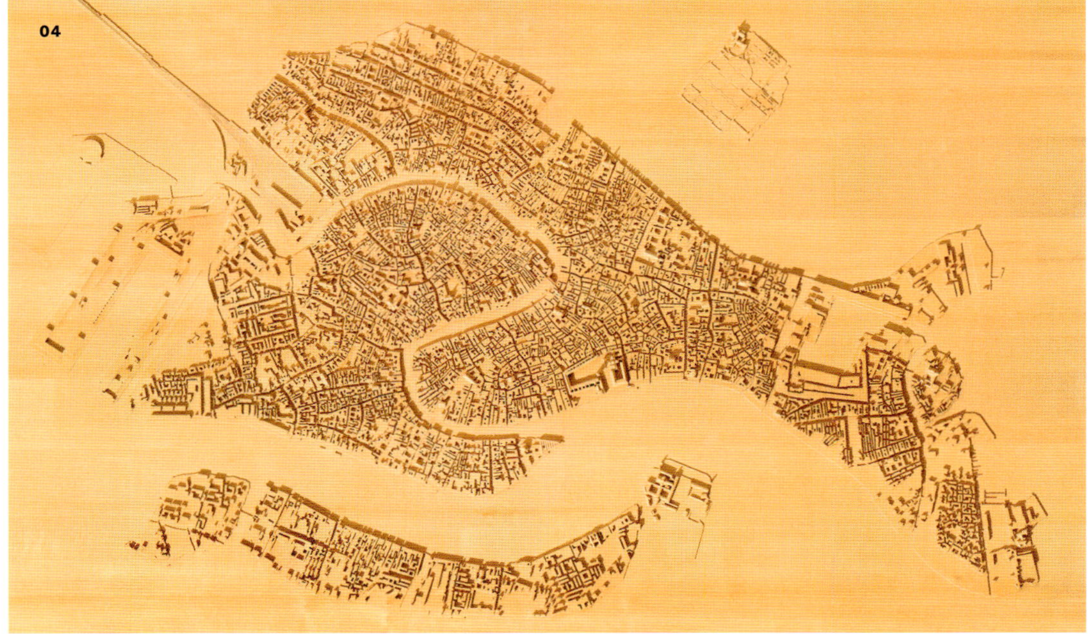

01 / 02

Berlin City Centre, Presentation model, 2006
Property of werner-modelle
Scale: 1:5,000
Material: Wild service tree wood (solid)
Photos: LEISKA

03 / 04

Venice, Italy, Presentation model
Client: Private
Scale: 1:5,000
Material: Wild service tree wood (solid)
Photos: LEISKA

01

Relief of the city of Hamburg
Scale: 1:2,000
Collaborator: Bernhard Ihle
Manual finishing and surface treatment are
essential to complete the city relief.

02

Since a wooden relief of a city stays on the machine for
weeks while it is being developed, some handwork has
to be performed in situ...

03

Detail: Hamburg HafenCity
Scale: 1:2,000
Material: Wild service tree wood (solid)
Work process: After rough machining

04

Detail: Hamburg, wholesale market halls
Scale: 1:2,000
Material: Wild service tree wood (solid)
Work process: After smoothing

The following staff members played
a part in the models shown here:
Dipl. Ing. Mark Blume,
Dipl. Ing. Bernhard Ihle,
Dipl. Ing. Norbert Freitag.

The Deutsche Bibliothek lists this publication in the
Deutsche Nationalbibliografie; detailed bibliographic
data is available on the internet at http://dnb.ddb.de

ISBN 978-3-938666-49-4

© 2008 by DOM publishers
www.dom-publishers.com

Editor
Uta Keil

Layout
Rüdiger Fandler, Berlin

Printed by
SNP Leefung, Shenzhen